the
approval
FIX

the approval FIX

How to Break Free from People Pleasing

JOYCE MEYER

New York   Boston   Nashville

Unless otherwise noted, all Scripture quotations are from *The Amplified Bible*.
Copyright © 1954, 1958, 1962, 1964, 1965, 1987 by The Lockman Foundation.
Used by permission.

Scripture quotations marked NKJV are from the New King James Version. Copyright © 1979, 1980, 1982 by Thomas Nelson, Inc. Used by permission. All rights
reserved.

Scripture quotations marked MSG are from THE MESSAGE. Copyright © by Eugene
H. Peterson, 1993, 1994, 1995. Used by permission of NavPress Publishing Group.

FaithWords
Hachette Book Group
237 Park Avenue
New York, NY 10017

www.faithwords.com

Printed in the United States of America

WOR

First Edition: June 2014
10 9 8 7 6

FaithWords is a division of Hachette Book Group, Inc.
The FaithWords name and logo are trademarks of Hachette Book Group, Inc.

The Hachette Speakers Bureau provides a wide range of authors for speaking events.
To find out more, go to www.hachettespeakersbureau.com or call (866) 376-6591.

The publisher is not responsible for websites (or their content) that are not
owned by the publisher.

Library of Congress Cataloging-in-Publication Data

Meyer, Joyce, 1943–
    The approval fix : how to break free from people pleasing / Joyce Meyer. —
First Edition.
        pages cm
    ISBN 978-1-4555-4715-9 (hardcover) — ISBN 978-1-4555-5327-3
(spanish-language trade pbk.) — ISBN 978-1-4789-5348-7 (audiobook) —
ISBN 978-1-4789-5349-4 (audio download) — ISBN 978-1-4555-5117-0 (ebook)
    1. God (Christianity)—Love. 2. Social acceptance. I. Title.
    BT140.M47 2014
    241'.4—dc23
                                                    2013041651

CONTENTS

INTRODUCTION

How many times have you heard or felt "You're approved!"? You may have heard it when applying for a job or trying to buy a home, or felt it when agreeing to marry the love of your life.

Often, we don't feel or hear that we are approved enough to cause us to believe it. Because we have not learned to rest in the fact that God approves of us all the time, many of us go through life feeling "wrong," inse-cure, or rejected somehow. We don't always love ourselves or feel that others really love, accept, or approve of us. The way we think about ourselves and the ways other people treat us cause us to lose our self-confidence and develop low self-esteem. This leaves us feeling empty and hungry inside, and we seek to satisfy ourselves by doing things we think will cause others to like us, affirm us, and approve of us. We end up with what I call "approval addiction."

I believe approval addiction is rampant in our society today. It is not limited to any certain age group, gender, or socioeconomic sphere. It can happen to anyone! When it does, people may feel insecure or rejected, and they may lose their unique, God-given sense of identity because they forsake their true personalities or don't develop their gifts in an effort to do and be what they believe others want them to do and be.

I know firsthand how negatively the desire for approval can affect people's lives, because I experienced it. Anyone who has been hurt badly through abuse or severe rejection, as I have, often seeks the approval of others to try to overcome feelings of rejection and low self-esteem. They suffer from those feelings and use their addiction to approval to try to relieve their pain. They are miserable if anyone seems not to approve of them in any way or for any reason, and they remain anxious about that disapproval until they feel accepted once again. They may do almost anything to gain the approval they feel they have lost—even things their consciences tell them are wrong. For example, if a person does not feel approved of when she declines an invitation, she might change her plans and accept the invitation simply to gain approval. She compromises herself for the sake of feeling approved. Unfortunately, people do things like this often; it's the only way they know how to feed their need for approval and to avoid feeling rejected.

The good news is that no one has to continue to try to find worth, validation, or value in other people's approval. No one needs to suffer any longer with insecurity or rejection.

Nobody has to strive to please others while being miserable doing so. There is a cure for the approval addiction! The Word of God says we can be secure through Jesus Christ (see Ephesians 3:17). That means we are free to be ourselves and to become all we can be in Him.

If you have found yourself addicted to approval, spending too much time and energy trying to get people to accept you, I believe this book can change your life in the most positive ways. The major change may not happen immediately, but the following pages include many proven principles that have helped thousands of people, including myself, break free from approval addiction. They also include a number of stories I believe you will identify with and from which you can learn valuable lessons for your life. I am living proof that a life filled with insecurity, rejection, fear, and pain can be transformed into a life of confidence, acceptance, love, peace, joy, and strength. Does that sound good to you? Then let's get started!

PART 1

Accepting Who You Are

CHAPTER

1

God Loves You

Carol was a miserable and frustrated young mother. She constantly compared herself to other people she knew and struggled to be like them. She wanted to be the cook her mother had been, the parent her friends were, and the wife her overly demanding husband expected her to be. She was a stay-at-home mom with three young children and had her hands full, but she often felt that perhaps she should also work a full-time job to help with the family finances. She was never relaxed, nor did she enjoy feeling confident.

She tried so hard to gain everyone's approval that she was mentally, emotionally, and physically exhausted most of the time. She feared the rejection of the people she loved, and she lived her life every day trying keep them happy, rather than following God and her own heart. She felt imprisoned by her fears, and she was in a trap she did not know how to break out of. Carol was also starting to feel bitter because she felt that other people's demands were stealing her life, but what was really stealing her life was her unwillingness to trust God and be bold enough to be the person He wanted her to be.

She wanted other people to change and be less demanding, but God wanted her to change and be bold enough to stand up to them when she needed to. We must all learn to stand up for our right to be ourselves and not cave in to the pressure we frequently feel to be someone that we truly don't know how to be.

Carol was searching for significance in all the wrong places. She kept trying to get from people what only God could give her, which was unconditional love and acceptance. The root of her problem was that she felt guilty and ashamed of herself due to some unresolved abuse in her childhood, and she needed emotional healing from God. No matter how many people she tried to please in her life, she would never feel whole and complete until she received Jesus as her Savior and learned to see herself through His eyes.

———

Do you relate to Carol? If so, I pray that you are ready to let Jesus set you free from the tyranny of being a people pleaser and an approval addict. Do you live under a burden of guilt or shame, feeling unworthy and insecure? Do you go through life feeling something is wrong with you but are unable to articulate what it is? Are you a people pleaser, always looking for the approval of others?

If so, those feelings affect every area of your life. They affect your personal relationships; since you are a Christian, they also adversely affect your prayer life, your ability to grow spiritually, and your pursuit of your God-given destiny. They certainly steal your joy, your peace, and your ability to look confidently toward your future— and that is not God's will for you. God wants you to live with confidence in His love for you, and to boldly do and be all that He has planned for you.

God's will is for you to enjoy your life and fulfill the purpose for which He created you. To live a life you enjoy, a life filled with purpose, you will need the confidence that comes from knowing you are right with God through Jesus, a healthy, positive self-image, and good relationships with others. These things cannot coexist with an approval addiction, so the addiction has to go.

The first step to understanding and breaking free from approval addiction is to understand fear, because fear of some sort is at the root of an unbalanced need for approval. People deal with an endless variety of fears, but one I discovered in my own life—and one you may also be dealing with—is the fear of not being pleasing to God. This is common among Christians who struggle with approval addiction.

If you have ever been hurt by someone who is difficult

or impossible to please, you may think God is the same way. He isn't! In fact, pleasing God is not nearly as hard as you may think. Simple, childlike faith pleases Him. He already knows we are not perfect and will not behave perfectly all the time. That is why He sent Jesus to pay for our failures and mistakes.

Believers Believe

For many years, I struggled in frustration trying to please God with good or even perfect behavior. At the same time, I was always afraid I was failing. No matter what I did right, I always seemed to find something I was doing wrong. I never felt good enough; regardless of how well I did certain things, I always felt I needed to do more. I thought God was displeased with me, and even though that was wrong, it was true for me because I believed it.

Many people, maybe even you, have believed lies that have kept them in bondage. They have been unable to break free and move into the great life God has for them simply because of wrong belief systems. If you have believed lies in the past, you can let them go, begin to believe truth, and enjoy the awesome future God has planned for you.

Christians are called *believers*. God accepts us because of our faith, not our good works. If our job were to achieve, we would be called *achievers*, not *believers*. We often want to emphasize what *we* do, but our focus should be on what *God* has done for us in Jesus Christ. We have a choice: we can concentrate on our sin and be miserable, or we can concentrate on God's forgiveness and mercy and be happy.

Once we see this truth, we can enjoy our relationship with God. We don't have to feel pressured to behave perfectly and then be afraid we have failed when our performance is less than perfect. If we want to please God with all our hearts, all we need to do is believe in His Son Jesus Christ and believe what He says in His Word.

It's a Trap!

Believing we must perform perfectly to be accepted is a snare of the enemy; it is not from God. I lived in the performance-acceptance trap for many years because I was addicted to approval. I felt if I performed well, then God and others would accept me and approve of me. I did not feel good about myself, nor did I accept myself unless my performance was admirable. When I did not perform well, I automatically assumed God rejected me, because experience had taught me to expect such behavior from the people around me and I believed God was just like they were. God does not reject us when we make mistakes, but if we *think* He does, if we *fear* He does, that lie becomes truth to us, because we believe it.

I once had an employee who had experienced much rejection from her father when she did not do well in school or perform perfectly in other areas. When she came to work for our ministry and her job performance was anything less than perfect, I sensed her withdrawing from me, and I felt she was rejecting me. Not only did she withdraw, she also went into a frenzy trying to get more work done. If I asked about the status of her work, she only seemed calm and happy if she could tell me everything was done, and done *exactly* right.

I did not understand my employee's behavior at the time, but through prayer and sharing openly we finally discovered that she was extremely afraid of being rejected if she did not perform perfectly. Thankfully, she eventually learned to believe I loved and accepted her even though her performance was not always perfect. This enabled us to work together in joy for many years.

Just as I had learned in my own life, my employee had to learn to believe what I said rather than what she felt. We must choose to do likewise in our relationship with God. We must learn to trust His Word more than our own feelings. We often bow down to our feelings without realizing how fickle and unreliable they are. God loves us and accepts us unconditionally. His love is not based on our performance; He does not "grade" us. Ephesians 1:6 says we are made acceptable in the Beloved (NKJV). Our faith in Jesus, not our performance, is what makes us acceptable to God and pleases Him.

Relax. God Is Pleased.

Anyone who loves God wants to please Him. The fact that we desire to please Him pleases Him. We want God's approval, and there is nothing wrong with that. In fact, a desire to please God is necessary because it motivates us to seek His will in all things. People who have a deep desire to please God may not perform perfectly all the time, but they keep pressing forward and continually want to improve. Their attitudes and motives are right before God, and that pleases Him.

Second Chronicles 16:9 says God is searching for someone in whom He can show Himself strong, someone whose heart is perfect toward Him. This verse does not say He is looking for someone with a perfect performance but for someone with a perfect heart—a heart that desires to please Him, a heart that grieves over sin and evil, a heart that believes in Him and in His willingness and ability to forgive and restore. God knows we cannot achieve perfection. If we could, we would be perfect in our performance; we would not need a Savior, and Jesus would have come in vain.

God is a God of hearts. He sees and cares about our attitudes of heart more than our performance.

You can relax and take comfort in the fact that God approves of you completely and is pleased with you. His approval and pleasure do not depend on you; they rest completely on the fact that you are in Christ and on everything Jesus has done for us. God is not surprised by your inabilities, your imperfections, or your faults. He has always known everything about you, things you are just now finding out, and He chose you on purpose for Himself. Jesus presents you blameless and faultless before God if you place your trust in Him (see 1 Corinthians 1:7–8). He loves you and values you more than you know!

CHAPTER
2

You Are Valuable

I come from an abusive background. My past left me suffering from insecurities even after I became a Christian because I was not seeing myself through the eyes of Scripture. I didn't like myself and rejected myself because I did not see myself as God saw me. I did not know who I was in Christ; I was not rooted and grounded in His love, and I did not know I could find my approval in Him. Even though Scripture told me I had been re-created in Christ (see Ephesians 2:10), made new, and given a fresh start and a great future, I still saw myself as a failure, someone unlovable and unacceptable.

My life was extremely difficult during that time. I was continually frustrated and had no real peace or joy, because I had a poor self-image and felt nobody liked me. Those feelings caused me to act as though I did not need anyone or care about how others thought or felt about me.

Yet deep inside, I really did care, and I tried very hard to be what others expected me to be.

But as I studied the Word of God, I learned I am valuable in who I am in Christ, not in what I do or in other people's opinions of me. I realized I did not have to stay insecure because when God looked at me, He saw the righteousness of His Son Jesus (see 2 Corinthians 5:21), not everything that was wrong with me or everything I had done wrong. That truth set me free, and it will do the same for you. For the first time in my life, I learned how important it was for me to fill my mind with the Word of God, and I felt secure.

It's All in Your Mind

Breaking an addiction begins in the mind, with getting established in the truth of God's Word. Whether people are addicted to something physical, such as drugs, alcohol, or gambling, or to something emotional, such as approval, they will never break its grip until they start thinking differently. A certain way of thinking got them into the addiction and keeps them there, so it makes sense that new thought patterns—such as focusing on their righteousness, not their "wrongness"—will help set them free from it. I encourage you to form a habit of being "righteousness conscious" rather than "sin conscious." Focus on Jesus and His love, forgiveness, and mercy toward you rather than on everything you have done wrong.

We can begin to change our thinking, which Scripture calls "renewing our minds," through studying God's Word (see Romans 12:2). As we think differently, we will behave differently because, as I like to say, "where the mind goes the man follows," meaning that our thoughts guide our actions (see Proverbs 23:7). Years ago, my thinking changed when I saw in God's Word that He was actually pleased with me and accepted me even though I did not behave perfectly. I purposefully started expecting people to like me. And sure enough, they did. I even began to confess aloud that God gave me favor and that people liked me. I learned to say what God says about me instead of what the enemy wants me to believe, and that is critical for anyone who wants to break free from any kind of bondage.

God tries to tell us in His Word how much He loves us and He accepts us, and that even though He already knows every mistake we will ever make, He still chose us for Himself. Ephesians 1:4 says:

Even as [in His love] He chose us [actually picked us out for Himself as His own] in Christ before the foundation of the world, that we should be holy (consecrated and set apart for Him) and blameless in His sight, even above reproach, before Him in love.

We read this truth, but we have difficulty receiving it. We let our feelings about ourselves steal the blessings of

God's acceptance and approval. We allow other people's opinions to determine our worth and value rather than relying on God's Word. If we will not only read the words of Scripture but also believe and embrace them, we will do ourselves a huge favor.

I encourage you to say aloud several times a day: "God loves me unconditionally, and He is pleased with me." The mind rejects such statements; after all, how could God, who is perfect, be pleased with us in our imperfections? The point is that God separates *who we are* from *what we do*. Let me explain.

My children are Meyers. They don't always act right, but they never stop being Meyers; they never stop being my children. Knowing their hearts are right goes a long way with me. They make mistakes, but as long as they admit them and their hearts are pure, I am always willing to work with them.

God feels the same about you. As a believer in Jesus Christ, you are His child. You may not always act the way He wants you to, but you never stop being His child. I will never give up on my children, and God will never give up on us!

God Is Not Surprised

We often act as though God is shocked to discover that we fail or make mistakes. The truth is: God has a big eraser, and He uses it to keep our records clean and clear. He already knows the thoughts that have not even crossed our minds yet and the words that have not crossed our lips. Even with all His foreknowledge of our weaknesses and mistakes, He still chose us on purpose and brought us into relationship with Himself through Christ.

If we never make mistakes, then we are probably not making many decisions. Our mistakes have value; we can learn from them. But we are often embarrassed about our mistakes or ashamed of our failures. We want to look good so others will think highly of us.

I am reminded of an anecdote I've heard several times. A well-known speaker started his seminar by holding up a $50 bill. He asked his audience, "Who would like this fifty-dollar bill?" Hands started going up.

He said, "I am going to give it to one of you, but first let me do this."

He proceeded to crumple the bill and then asked, "Who still wants it?"

The hands went back up.

"Well," he replied, "what if I do this?" And he dropped it on the ground and started to grind it into the floor with his shoe. He picked it up, creased, crumpled, and dirty.

"Now who still wants it?" he asked the crowd. Hands remained in the air.

"My friends, you have all learned a valuable lesson. No matter what I did to the money, you still wanted it because it did not decrease in value. It was still worth fifty dollars."

Many times in our lives, the circumstances we face or the decisions we make cause us to feel we have been dropped, crushed, or ground into the dirt. We feel worthless. But no matter what has happened or what will happen, we will never lose our value in God's eyes. Dirty or clean, crumpled or finely creased, we are still priceless to Him.

Our desire for approval can truly be met only by receiving God's acceptance and approval of us. We cannot earn His love, we cannot buy His love, we cannot behave well enough to warrant God's love, and we cannot perform perfectly enough to merit it. All we can do with God's love is receive it as a gift, which it is—a gift to us through Jesus Christ. He has made us right with God!

You're Right!

One of the greatest cures for approval addiction is the knowledge of who we are in Christ. According to 2 Corinthians 5:21, we have been made the righteousness of God in Christ. The phrase "in Christ" is one we must understand if we are to go through life with strength and victory. Who we are in Christ is totally different from who we are in ourselves. In and of ourselves we are absolutely nothing of any value, but "in Christ" we partake of everything He deserved and earned. The Bible even says we are "joint heirs" with Christ (see Romans 8:17). In Him, we share His inheritance, His righteousness, and His holiness.

We need to learn to identify ourselves with Christ and to see ourselves as "in Him." We may use an analogy to better understand what it means to be "in Christ": If we were to place two pennies in a jar, seal the jar, and submerge it in water, the pennies would be in the water just as much as the jar is. Actually, though, the pennies would be better off because they would be in the same place as the jar but they would not get wet.

In the analogy of the jar, Jesus is the jar and we are the pennies. Everyone who believes in Jesus Christ is considered to be "in Him." Everything Jesus went through, we share. Even though we have not actually endured every single thing He experienced, all that He accomplished becomes ours through our faith in Him.

A lack of understanding about righteousness—or "rightness" with God—can result in an approval addiction and other bondages that leave us miserable. But once we understand how God sees us through Christ, we can be free from caring what people think about us and from feeling badly about ourselves. We don't have to be addicted to anyone's approval, because we already have God's complete, unconditional acceptance. We can stop living under condemnation and we can begin to accept ourselves. We can know God is pleased with us and that because we are in Christ, we are righteous.

How God Sees You

One of the most powerful Scriptures on the subject of righteousness is 2 Corinthians 5:21. I hope you will take time to read it, think about it and ask God to help you live every day in its truth:

For our sake He made Christ [virtually] to be sin
Who knew no sin, so that in and through Him we
might become [endued with, viewed as being in,
and examples of] the righteousness of God [what
we ought to be, approved and acceptable and in
right relationship with Him, by His goodness].

Notice that this verse says God *views* us as righteous.
That means He has decided to look at us in a certain way.
Ephesians 1:5 says He loved us and through Jesus Christ
adopted us as His own children, and that He did so "in
accordance with the purpose of His will [*because it pleased
Him and was His kind intent*]" (emphasis mine). In other
words, God loves us because He wants to, not because of
anything we can do to earn or merit His love. Since He is
God, He can do anything He wants to do, and He needs no
one's permission to do it. He has chosen to love us.

We may wonder why God would love us, because we
look at ourselves and can find no reason for Him to do so.
God does not have to be reasonable, because He is God!
The fact that we cannot understand what God does, does
not stop Him from doing it. We understand God with our
hearts, not with our heads. We may not know intellectu-
ally why God loves us, but we can know in our hearts that
He does. People usually need a reason to love and accept
us, but God does not.

Being righteous does not mean we are so perfect that

we have no weaknesses or flaws. It means we believe, according to 2 Corinthians 5:21, that Jesus became sin through His death on the cross, and that in becoming sin for us, He made us righteous. He actually took our sin upon Himself and paid the penalty for it. Being righteous is a state into which God places us, by His grace, through our faith in what Jesus did for us.

We need a "righteousness consciousness," an awareness that Jesus has made us righteous, not a "sin consciousness," which would keep us focused on our sins and shortcomings. We need to remember that God is not against us; He is on our side!

CHAPTER

4

God Is on Your Side

As believers, no matter what we do, we can be confident that God is on our side. The apostle Paul wrote in Romans 8:31: "What then shall we say to [all] this? If God is for us, who [can be] against us? [Who can be our foe, if God is on our side?]"

God is for us! That's great news! But the enemy is against us. The question we must ask ourselves is: are we going to agree with God or with the devil? You know the answer. You want to agree with God. And God is for you, so stop being against yourself just because the enemy is against you!

Sad to say, sometimes we discover that people are also against us. Satan sometimes works against us independently, but he often works through people as well. He attacks our confidence through things people say or don't say. Sometimes he inspires other people's opinions, judgments, and attitudes toward us. When that happens, we must resist and refuse to agree with them. Because we know the enemy can influence other people's thoughts and words, we really need to learn to think for ourselves under the leading of the Holy Spirit, not to seek the opinions and approval of others.

Most of us, to some extent, need to be delivered from the fear of other people. We need to be completely set free from caring what others think. People who constantly need approval desperately want everybody to look at everything they do—the way they look, the things they say, every action they take—and to say, "Perfect." We need to give God our reputation and let Him be in charge of it from now on. After all, He can do anything, and He is for us!

Clean and Fresh

As I mentioned, God can do anything, and one thing He does is wash off all our feelings of guilt or "wrongness." First John 1:9 teaches that if we admit our sins and confess them, God will forgive us and cleanse us from all unrighteousness.

Start by freely admitting your faults. Admit them to God and to trustworthy people. Don't make excuses or place blame elsewhere. As you do this, you will experience a new freedom, and your relationships with God and with other people will improve greatly. Don't feel you must hide your faults from God. He knows all about them anyway, so invite Him into every area of your life. Actually, the Lord knows more about us than we can remember or will ever discover, and He loves us anyway.

Give God not only what you are but especially give Him what you are not. Don't hold anything back; give Him everything! Offering God our strengths is easy, but we should also offer Him our weaknesses, because His strength is made perfect in our weaknesses. The Lord doesn't see only what we are right now, He sees what we can become if He is patient with us. He knows the plans He has for us, and they are plans for progress and success, not for defeat and failure (see Jeremiah 29:11).

A thorough and complete confession of our sins gives us a good, clean, fresh feeling. We might compare it to a closet that has been closed up for a long time and is full of junk and dirt. Once someone cleans it completely—throws away the junk, removes the dirt, and lets in fresh air—it becomes a pleasant place. We can enjoy ourselves and feel fresh and clean once we have completely confessed our sins and received God's forgiveness for them.

God Will Give You Confidence

Understanding that we are forgiven and cleansed, and knowing who we are in Christ sets us free from the need to impress others. As long as we know who we are, we don't have to be overly concerned about what others think of us. Once we know who we are and accept ourselves, we no longer have anything to prove. When we have nothing to prove we can relax and be at ease in every situation.

Knowing who we are in Christ will also help us be confident, and as a result others will be drawn to us; people tend to gravitate toward those who are confident and secure. We cannot make ourselves acceptable to everyone, but we can believe God will give us favor with the people with whom He wants us to be involved. Sometimes we try to have relationships with people with whom God does not even want us to be associated. Some of the people I worked hard to be friends with in the past, often compromising my own conscience to gain their acceptance, were the very ones who rejected me the first time I didn't do exactly as they wanted me to do. I realize now that I wanted their friendship for the wrong reasons. I was insecure and wanted to be friends with the "popular" people, thinking my association with "important" people would make me important.

People look for qualities in others that will make them feel better, safe, and secure. We can deal with people fearfully or we can deal with them confidently. We are to be confident but we are not to place our confidence in anyone or anything other than Christ Himself. Knowing our position in Him gives us confidence, and as a result people will desire friendship with us. Confident people never lack for friends because they have what everyone wants. They have assurance and confidence, they have worth and value, and they are secure.

CHAPTER
5

You'll Become What You Believe

When we accept by faith and receive personally the truth that we are the righteousness of God, we begin to conform to what we believe we are. This keeps us from being ruled by what other people say or think about us.

The Amplified Bible describes righteousness as being made right with God and then consistently conforming to His will in word, thought, and deed (see Romans 10:3). In other words, when we are made right with God, we begin to think right, we begin to talk right, and we begin to act right. This is a process in which we are continually making progress. The outworking of righteousness—ultimately seen in right thoughts, words, and actions—cannot begin until we *accept* our right standing with God through Jesus Christ. The starting point is the moment we believe we are the righteousness of God in Christ, according to 2 Corinthians 5:21. I encourage you to speak aloud what

God says about you in His Word. Say daily, "I am the righteousness of God in Christ, and therefore I can produce right behavior."

Thinking Right

Ask yourself what you believe about yourself. Do you believe you must have people's approval in order to be happy? If so, you will never be happy when anyone disapproves of you. Do you believe you are all wrong? If you do, you will continue to produce wrong behavior. The fruit of your life is directly connected to your beliefs about yourself. You will become what you believe you are.

Our righteousness is not found in what people think of us; it is found in Christ. He is our righteousness from God. Romans 5:17 assures us:

> For if because of one man's trespass (lapse, offense) death reigned through that one, much more surely will those who receive [God's] overflowing grace (unmerited favor) and the free gift of righteousness [putting them into right standing with Himself] reign as kings in life through the one Man Jesus Christ (the Messiah, the Anointed One).

We must learn to think about and believe in our righteousness.

Speaking Right

"Words are powerful; take them seriously. Words can be your salvation. Words can also be your damnation" (Matthew 12:37, MSG).

One way we learn to talk right is to be careful what we say about ourselves.

I know a young lady I'll call Susan. Susan loves the Lord, but she comes from an abusive background. She is very insecure and a real people pleaser. I would definitely say she is an approval addict. Susan lets people control her much of the time. She says what she thinks people want to hear instead of speaking honestly, from her heart. Susan goes to church; she hears a lot of teaching about rules, regulations, and church doctrine, but not much about how to live her life in strength and power. This means she does not understand the importance of words, especially her own words. She does not realize her words are keeping her weak and defeated in life. Susan needs to learn to think and speak according to God's Word so she can enjoy God's good plan for her life.

Many of us are like Susan, unaware of how powerful our words are. We need to learn to speak positively and victoriously. We need to learn to say by faith about ourselves what God says about us in His Word.

Acting Right

If we are going to represent Jesus properly, we need to live with strength and power to overcome everything that comes against us. We are more than conquerors, according to Romans 8:37. If we are defeated and lack victory, no one will want what we have. But when we are victorious, others see it and want the same in their lives. To put it plainly, if we want other people to accept Jesus, we must show them that having a relationship with Him makes a real difference in our lives. When we call ourselves Christians and go to church but repeatedly behave badly, people think we are hypocrites and phonies. The way we act is important! God has given us the power to make right choices and to demonstrate right behavior.

In 1976, the realization that I was a Christian with very little victory urged me to seek a deeper relationship with God. As a Christian, I knew I was saved by grace and that I would go to heaven when I died, but I was not enjoying the journey. I was miserable; I had a negative attitude and a negative life. I needed a big change. As I pursued a deeper relationship with God through His Word, I realized He had a much better life for me than I ever dreamed; my actions improved and my life got better. I know God has the same for you.

Don't settle for anything less than the best God has to offer you. You can have a deep, intimate, personal relationship with God through Jesus Christ. You can enjoy daily fellowship with Him and walk in power every day as you allow Him to teach you how to live, how to think, how to talk, and how to act for your own good and happiness, as well as to glorify Him.

Forgiven and Free

As you grow more and more in your awareness of your righteousness in Christ, you will begin to need other people's approval less and less. Even though you have been made righteous and you are learning to think, speak, and act rightly, you will still sin. We all do. But thankfully we can all receive forgiveness and keep growing into the fullness of what God desires us to become.

One morning I was spending time with the Lord, thinking about my problems and all the areas in which I had failed, when suddenly, the Lord asked me a question: "Joyce, are you going to fellowship with Me or with your problems?"

I had definitely been "fellowshipping" with my problems! I was more focused on them and on how bad I felt about them than on God and the fact that He wanted to forgive me of my sins and help me solve my problems.

Our fellowship and union with God strengthens us and helps us to overcome our problems. If we spend our time with God fellowshipping with our previous mistakes, we never receive strength to overcome them today. Focusing on our faults and failures weakens us, but meditating on God's grace and willingness to forgive strengthens us:

> *For by the death He died, He died to sin [ending His relation to it] once for all; and the life that He lives, He is living to God* [in unbroken fellowship with Him]. *Even so consider yourselves also dead to sin and your relation to it broken, but alive to God* [living in unbroken fellowship with Him] *in Christ Jesus.*
> —Romans 6:10–11 (emphases mine)

How much do you fellowship with your sins, failures, mistakes, and weaknesses? Whatever time it is, it is wasted. When you sin, admit it, ask for forgiveness, and then continue your fellowship with God. Don't let your sins come between you and the Lord. Even when you sin, God still wants to spend time with you, hear and answer your prayers, and help you with all of your needs. He wants you to run *to* Him, not *away* from Him.

Just Be Yourself

I hope you can see that the fact you are a Christian does not mean you will do everything right all the time. But because you have been made right with God, you can stop comparing yourself to others and competing with them. Your acceptance is not found in being like someone else, but in being who you are through faith in Jesus Christ. Don't find someone who seems to have it all together and then try your best to be like they are. Be the best "you" that you can be!

We all have baggage and issues we try to hide in public. Despite how wonderful certain people may appear to others, we *all* make mistakes. You are no worse than anyone else. You have strengths and weaknesses; you do things right and you do things wrong. You sin, just as everyone else does. And sin is sin, despite its nature or magnitude. God's Word teaches us in Romans 6 that we are free from the power of sin. I don't believe that means that we never sin, but that we are free from the guilt and condemnation of sin. It is wonderful to realize that every mistake we make was already paid for by Jesus when He died on the cross. His provision is available, and all we need to do is admit our sin, turn from it, and receive God's amazing grace.

———

Regardless of how hard we try, none of us will ever be completely perfect in this life, but not being perfect at everything we do does not mean we have no worth or value.

You are special—unique—and that means there is only one like you, imperfections and all. Please remember that you don't have to be like someone else to be acceptable. The world's standards are not God's. The world may say you need to be like this person or that person, but God's will is for you to be yourself.

Jesus is our standard, not any other person. If you are going to seek to be like anyone, let it be Jesus Himself. He is our righteousness, so believe and embrace the righteousness He gives you. You'll become what you believe.

CHAPTER

6

God Has the Right Position for You

Have you ever interviewed for a job and been told that it seems to be just the right position for you? Or maybe you have had the opposite experience, believing you would do well in a certain role, but having someone in authority say, "We don't think it's a fit. This is not the right position for you." Both situations teach us that we can be in right positions or wrong positions in life.

As believers, the right position for us is in Christ. That is where we find unconditional love, acceptance, and approval. But until we understand and embrace that truth, many of us spend valuable time and energy seeking validation and approval in positions the world offers: social positions, professional positions, and other positions that seem impressive to people around us but actually fail to give us what we really need.

The Power of Position

I think insecurity and the need for approval are two main reasons people struggle for position and power. They derive their sense of worth and value from what they do rather than from who they are. This is why some people become approval addicts, always needing the approval of others to be happy and secure. It is also why some people are so competitive and think, *I have to win*. To feel valuable, they must be the best, finish first, or hold some kind of position that makes them feel powerful.

I remember *really* wanting a specific position in a church I attended years ago. I knew that to get the position a certain group of people would have to like me and accept me, because they had the power to vote me into the position or keep me out of it. I gave those individuals compliments, sent them gifts, and extended them invitations to dinner. I did and said all the "right" things until I finally got what I thought I wanted.

After getting the position, I soon discovered that if I did not allow the people who voted me into that role to control me, they could be very vindictive. I wanted the position because at that time I needed it to feel valuable and important, yet it ended up making me feel miserable and manipulated.

My story illustrates the point that whatever we gain by the works of our flesh, we must maintain through efforts of the flesh. In my church position, as soon as I did a few things the "powerful" people did not like, they all rejected me. Our entire relationship was phony; they did not really like me or care about me, and I really did not like or care about them.

That position could never make me feel permanently secure and approved of, because the real problem was inside of me, not in my circumstances. I did not need a position; I needed a revelation of God's unconditional love. I needed to seek God's approval, not people's approval. I needed to know that I was valuable to God as a person totally apart from any position I might hold.

Find Your Place in God

Until we accept and approve of ourselves, no amount of approval from others or position in life will keep us permanently secure. The outside approval we seek becomes an addiction. We work to get approval and it feels good for a short while; then we find that we need more and more. True freedom never comes until we fully realize that we don't need to struggle to get from others what God freely gives us: love, acceptance, approval, security, worth, and value.

I encourage you not to let your value become attached to a position. Positions can come and go in life, but God and His love for you remain. God is not impressed with the positions people hold (see Galatians 2:6). If we know who we are in Christ, then we can have a healthy self-image apart from any position or job title. If we wait for God to promote us into the positions He wants us to have, then we can truly enjoy them, because when God puts us somewhere He also enables us to be there without struggle and frustration.

Quite some time after my experience wanting the church position I ultimately got and did not enjoy, I held a position with a different church in St. Louis, Missouri, and I held it for many years. When God led me to let it go and start my own ministry, I had a difficult time being obedient; and the longer I remained disobedient, the more miserable I became. I liked my position. I had a title, a parking place with my name on it, a guaranteed seat in the front row of the church, and everyone's admiration. I always knew what was going on. I actually did not realize how dependent I was on the position to give me feelings of security until God told me to walk away from it.

I finally did obey God, but the feelings I experienced after I left the position shook me to the core. I still attended that church, but I felt out of place every time I went to a service. I no longer had a seat or a parking place, and I knew nothing about all kinds of things that were happening. I didn't know where I belonged anymore. God had to teach me that my place is in Him, and that as long as I know that, I don't have to be uncomfortable anywhere with anyone.

Keep God First

Have you ever had an experience like mine, when you felt like all the props in your life were kicked out from under you? If so, consider that God may have done you a huge favor. Sometimes people or positions prop us up, and the only way we realize how much we depend on them is to have them removed.

A prop is something that holds something else in place, that makes another object secure. God wants our security to be in Him, not in anything else. He is the only thing in life that is not shaky, the only thing certain and sure. God allows some "props" in our lives while we are getting established in Him, but eventually He removes everything we depend on excessively. This frightens us initially, but it ends up being the best thing that ever happened to us. When we don't have anything or anyone else, we develop a deep relationship with God that will carry us through anything life brings our way.

If you feel you have lost something or someone you cannot do without, you are wrong. The only thing or person in life we absolutely cannot do without is God. He is our Strength, our Stronghold in times of trouble, our High Tower, our Hiding Place, and our Refuge (see Psalm 9:9; 31:4; 32:7; 37:39; 46:11).

When I lost the people I thought were my friends and again when I lost my position at the church, I hurt so much emotionally I thought I would not survive. Looking back, I can now say these events actually helped me realize that I depended entirely too much on my position, on other people, and on their opinions of me. I thought if I had a high position then people would think well of me and accept me.

When we need positions or anything else the world offers in order to feel good about ourselves, God often withholds or removes those things. Once we no longer *need* them, He can give them to us, because they will not control us. Now I have friends, influence, position, authority, acceptance, and other things I enjoy, but the key to keeping them is knowing beyond a shadow of doubt that I don't have to have them to be happy and fulfilled.

I am convinced that as long as we keep God first in our lives, He will give us everything else (see Matthew 6:33). I strongly encourage you to be careful not to let anything become more important to you than it should be. Keep God first, and you will be headed toward a great and successful future!

CHAPTER
7

You Have a Promising Future

Succeeding at something usually makes people feel good, or even great, about themselves. Failing at something, or believing they have failed, can make people feel bad about themselves. When people fail, they often feel unworthy, unintelligent, or unwise, devalued, rejected, and/or hopeless. These feelings cause people to crave approval. If you have failed at something, as we *all* do, I hope this chapter will encourage you greatly. You have good reasons to be filled with hope!

Failing Does Not Make You a Failure

One great reason for hope is this: you are not a failure just because you have failed at certain things. Nobody is good at everything. Don't let previous mistakes damage or distort your self-image. Sometimes the only way we can find out what we are meant to be doing in life is to step out and try some things. If they don't go well, we can still learn from them.

When I was seeking God's will for my life in ministry, I tried working in the church nursery. It didn't even take two weeks to know that position was not my ministry. I knew it, and so did the children! I also tried street ministry, and although I did it, I was very uncomfortable and actually disliked it very much. At first I felt guilty for not wanting to go out and tell people about Jesus, but I later realized that if God had intended that type of ministry for me, He would have given me a gift and desire in that area. I once worked as secretary to my pastor, and I got fired the first day. Just because I failed at that job does not mean I am a failure; I have gone on to be quite successful.

No matter how you have failed in the past or what mistakes you have made, you, too, can move beyond them and enjoy a life of blessing and success.

Getting Past Your Past

A lot of people let the past—especially the mistakes or failures of their pasts—dictate their future. Don't do that! Get past your past. We all have a past, but we also all have a future. Ephesians 2:10 says we are re-created in Christ Jesus so we might do the good works He prearranged and made ready for us. We are new creatures when we enter into a relationship with Christ. Old things pass away. We have an opportunity for a new beginning. We become new spiritual clay for the Holy Spirit to work with. God makes arrangements for each of us to have fresh start, but we must be willing to let go of the past and move on. We make a way for a new and better future by believing what God says about it: "For I know the thoughts and plans that I have for you, says the Lord, thoughts and plans for welfare and peace and not for evil, to give you hope in your final outcome" (Jeremiah 29:11).

The enemy wants us to have negative attitudes and to feel hopeless, but God's Word says we should be "prisoners of hope" (Zechariah 9:12). Don't ever stop hoping. Don't let your past failures leave you hopeless about your future success. Your future has no room in it for the failures of the past. As I have stated, you may have failed at some things, but that does not make you a failure. Regardless of your mistakes, God will heal and restore you if you are willing to press forward, forgetting the past. You have to let go in order to go on!

Refuse to Stop Trying

One way to go on is to refuse to stop trying. Some people the world sees as most successful experienced failure numerous times. Abraham Lincoln lost several elections before he was elected president of the United States. As a matter of fact, he ran for public office so many times and failed so often it's hard to understand how he had the nerve to run again. Yet, he did—and won.

Thomas Edison reportedly once said: "I failed my way to success." He refused to stop trying, and he finally invented the first practical lightbulb, but he succeeded only after thousands of failed experiments. A person like Edison who will not give up is an individual of strong character.

I personally believe failure is part of every real success, because failing our way to success humbles us. It is a vital part of God's being able to use us effectively.

A man named Charles Darrow set a goal when he was in his twenties: he determined to be a millionaire. That isn't unusual today, but during the 1920s it was extremely unusual, and a million dollars was an enormous sum. He married a woman named Esther, promising her that one day they would be millionaires.

In 1929, tragedy struck: the Great Depression. Both Charles and Esther lost their jobs. They mortgaged their house, gave up their car, and used all their life's savings. Charles was crushed. He sat around the house depressed until one day he told his wife she could leave him if she wanted to. "After all," he said, "it's clear we're never going to reach our goal." Esther wasn't about to leave. She told Charles they *were* going to reach their goal, but they needed to do something every day to keep their dream alive.

When Esther Darrow told her husband: "Keep your dream alive," Charles responded: "It's dead. We failed. Nothing's going to work." But she wouldn't listen to that kind of talk; she refused to believe it. She suggested that every night they take some time to discuss what they would do toward reaching their dream. They began doing this night after night, and soon Charles came up with the idea of creating play money. His idea was quite appealing, since money was so scarce in those days. Since they were both out of work, he and Esther had lots of time, and now had lots of easy money to play with. So they pretended to buy things like houses, property, and buildings. Soon they turned the fantasy into a full-fledged game with board, dice, cards, little houses, hotels…

You guessed it. It was the beginning of a game you probably have in your closet right now. It's called Monopoly.

What about You?

I pray you have been encouraged through the truths and stories in this chapter, and that if you have ever been discouraged because of failure, you are now filled with hope and courage. Just as Abraham Lincoln, Thomas Edison, and Charles Darrow refused to give up, you, too, must never stop trying. I often say my greatest testimony in life is that "I am still here." I didn't quit and give up, even though I certainly felt like doing so thousands of times.

God wants you to press on past mistakes; the enemy wants you to give up. Progress requires paying a price, and sometimes the price is just to "keep on keeping on" and saying, "I'm not going to quit until I have some kind of victory." Don't be the kind of person whose way of dealing with everything hard is "I quit!"

God has a great plan for your life, and He wants you to fulfill it. If you make mistakes or encounter failure along the way, learn your lessons and then get up the next day and try again. God loves you, He wants you to love yourself, and He has a bright future in store for you!

CHAPTER
8

Like Yourself, Love Yourself

A lot of people don't like themselves, but they don't realize it until I ask them about it. They don't know how they feel about themselves at all because they have never taken time to think about it. They should, though, because we all have a relationship with ourselves. We have to be with ourselves all the time. If we can't get along with ourselves, life can be quite miserable.

So let me ask you: how do you feel about yourself? If you have realized you don't like yourself, or that you don't like certain things about yourself, God wants to help you change your self-image. He wants you to feel great about who you are and to value yourself as He values you. We don't have to feel good about everything we do in order to feel good about ourselves.

The Bible teaches us to love our neighbors as we love ourselves (see Matthew 22:39). What if we don't love ourselves? That renders us incapable of loving others, which

is a big problem. What separates Christians from everyone else in the world is our love. Jesus said: "I give you
a new commandment: that you should love one another.
Just as I have loved you, so you too should love one
another. By this shall all [men] know that you are My disciples, if you love one another [if you keep on showing
love among yourselves]" (John 13:34–35).

People who cannot love themselves and approve of themselves live in emotional pain. If they don't approve of themselves, they may end up with excessive needs for approval
from others. Because of their excessive neediness and the
pressure it places on relationships, people may reject them.
God has created us not for rejection but for acceptance, and
we must receive His acceptance by accepting ourselves.

People who reject and even hate themselves are headed
for unhappy, frustrating lives. If you don't believe this,
just think about a time when you had to spend a day or
longer with someone you absolutely did not like or perhaps even really despised. It was likely a miserable time,
one you would avoid repeating. Not liking yourself basically fosters those same feelings! As God's creation, you
were made not to hate yourself but to love yourself and to
enjoy the good life God has given you.

Just Enjoy Yourself

Enjoying life is impossible if we don't enjoy ourselves.
You might ask, "Joyce, how can I enjoy myself? I do too

many dumb things and make too many mistakes to enjoy myself." Perhaps you don't like the way you look, or your personality, or even a particular feature of your body.

If that is the case, I understand. For many years I disliked my voice so much that I was almost paranoid about it. I actually dreaded opening my mouth and letting someone hear me speak for the first time, because I felt my voice was not one a woman should have. If you have ever heard me speak, you know my voice is very deep for a female. Quite often when I make phone calls, people who don't know me think I am a male. They call me Mr. Meyer. There were times when that made me angry, embarrassed me, and added to my feelings of insecurity.

The interesting thing is that my voice is what God is using most. He has chosen to use me in a media ministry through which my voice is heard daily in most of the world. God can take what we think is a flaw and do great things with it. As a matter of fact, He delights in doing just that. He shows Himself strong through what we would discard as having zero value.

What don't you like about yourself? Be specific; take an inventory and make a decision today to develop a new and more positive attitude toward yourself.

Jesus died so we could have life and enjoy it (see John 10:10). Living with daily self-rejection or self-hatred is a horrible way to live. We project to others the way we feel about ourselves. If we want other people to have good opinions of us, we must begin by having good opinions of ourselves and we must rest in the fact that God loves us. Having a good opinion of yourself doesn't mean that you are prideful; it means you have learned to see yourself as God sees you.

A Healthy Assessment of Yourself

People can stay trapped in low self-esteem or a poor self-image because they are afraid of appearing to be proud if they think highly of themselves or speak positively about themselves. The Bible does teach us not to have an exaggerated opinion of our own importance (see Romans 12:3). We are to esteem ourselves according to the grace of God, knowing that our strengths come from Him and do not make us better than others. We all have strengths and weaknesses. God says He gives gifts to everyone, and He chooses who will receive which ones (see 1 Corinthians 12:4–11).

Knowing that our gifts come from God, we are not to look down on someone who does not excel at the same things we do. We definitely need to avoid pride and remain humble, but we also need to keep from going to the other extreme and thinking self-rejection, self-hatred, and self-abasement are the answer.

Instead, seek to be what I call an "everything-nothing" person—everything in Christ and nothing without Him. Jesus Himself said, "Apart from Me you can do nothing" (John 15:5). Be confident, but remember that the strength that comes from confidence can quickly be lost in conceit. Loving yourself in a balanced, healthy way is godly and totally biblical.

In and of ourselves we can claim nothing good. Only God is good, and whatever good thing comes from us is merely a manifestation of His working through us (see Matthew 19:17).

Be Confident in Christ

If you have a critical, faultfinding attitude toward yourself, it is not only unhealthy, it is also not God's will. Paul refused to judge himself, and he paid no attention to anyone else who judged him: "But [as for me personally] it matters very little to me that I should be put on trial by you [on this point], and that you or any other human tribunal should investigate and question and cross-question me. I do not even put myself on trial and judge myself" (1 Corinthians 4:3).

Paul was confident in Christ. Because he knew he was acceptable to God in Christ, he accepted himself. He also knew who he was in Christ. He knew where he came from, and he knew where he was headed. I am sure Paul remembered his past and how he vehemently persecuted Christians prior to his conversion to Christ. He said himself that he had to make an effort to let go of the past and press on toward perfection. He also clarified that he did not think he had arrived (see Philippians 3:12–14).

In other words, Paul did not claim perfection, but neither did he have a bad attitude toward himself; he had an honest, healthy attitude. He knew he made mistakes, but he did not reject and despise himself because of them.

God wants so much to see us free and able to enjoy life that He was willing to send His only Son to die for these things (see John 3:16). He purchased our freedom with the blood of His Son. The least we can do is learn to see ourselves the way He sees us—precious and valuable.

Are you depressed, discouraged, and despondent? Do you spend so much time thinking about all of your faults that you have lost your hope and enthusiasm about living a good life? If so, please make a change today. Choose a new attitude toward yourself. Paul had to make that choice, I had to make it, and you must make it also if you want to glorify God with your life. The first step toward having a positive attitude toward yourself and learning to love yourself is to honestly address the issues that have caused you to dislike yourself and to want other people's approval excessively.

PART 2

Breaking Approval Addiction

CHAPTER
9

Turn the Light On

When people crave the approval of others, they work hard to hide their mistakes, faults, and flaws. They do this to appear as though they have it all together, so to speak, so they will be acceptable to others. The reason for such behavior often has its roots in the fear of being rejected or in the fear of not winning the approval of people they want to impress. When we look realistically at life and at people, we know that *everyone* has shortcomings. Often, trying to hide or disguise our flaws becomes a much bigger problem than the faults themselves could ever be. As we break free from approval addiction, we must understand the importance of bringing everything about ourselves—flaws and all—out of secrecy, where it only festers and gets worse, and into the open, where we can deal with it successfully. I have found in my ministry to others that one thing they truly appreciate is transparency. People want to be able to relate to us as being real and genuine. Being honest about our shortcomings usually brings us closer to people rather than separating us from them, as we fear it will.

Light Is Good!

When someone turns on a light in a dark room, we can see the dirt in it. God is light (see 1 John 1:5) and when His light begins to shine in our lives, it exposes things (see 1 Corinthians 4:5). When He gets involved in our lives, He begins to show us things we may prefer not to look at, things we have kept hidden, even from ourselves. We are frequently deceived, especially about ourselves. We prefer not to deal with our faults, and we do not enjoy having them exposed. When our weaknesses or mistakes are hidden, we may feel condemned about them, but at least we feel no one else can see them. Anything hidden has power over us because we fear it may be found out. The best and most freeing decision we can make is to choose to face up to what God wants to expose and get beyond the fear of it.

For many years I hid the fact that I had been sexually abused by my father. I saw it as a weakness, something to be ashamed of. I felt as though something was wrong with me. Because I was afraid of anyone knowing about my past, it continued to have power over me. When the Holy Spirit began leading me to share the details of my abusive past, I would shake violently. I was terribly afraid of my past. What would people think? Would they reject me? Would they blame me or hate me? The enemy had lied to me for at least twenty-five years about how people would view me if they knew about my past, so I worked hard to keep it a secret.

If someone asked me about my childhood, I avoided mentioning anything that might cause suspicion. I often told lies about my past and my parents. But when the truth about my past finally came into the light, the exact opposite of what I thought would happen took place. People responded with compassion, not with judgment. As I began to face my fears and talk about what had happened to me, my testimony began helping other people who were also locked in prisons of fear. The more I shared my past, the less power it had over me. God's light exposed Satan's lies, and the truth made me free.

Deal with It

Just as I learned to do, I encourage you to expose everything about your life to the light of God's love. We know that God chooses and uses people with flaws. Refusing to admit that we have faults may disqualify us from being used by God. He wants truth, not deception. He wants us to be truthful with Him, with ourselves, and with others. The apostle Paul wrote: "Let our lives lovingly express truth [in all things, speaking truly, dealing truly, living truly]. Enfolded in love, let us grow up in every way and in all things into Him Who is the Head, [even] Christ (the Messiah, the Anointed One)" (Ephesians 4:15).

When we refuse to embrace and love truth, we prevent our own spiritual growth. Whatever we refuse to deal with holds us in bondage. Some things are buried so deep that we don't consciously think about them, but they eat away at our lives like an infection.

I walked away from my father's house when I was eighteen years old. I had planned to do so for many years. I knew for years that I would leave when I graduated high school and was able to get a job to support myself. It was the only way I knew to get away from the abuse I had endured for so long. I walked away from the problem thinking it was over, not realizing it still existed in my soul.

I spent years hiding it, refusing to talk about it or even think about it, but that did not prevent me from having problems related to it. The infection grew daily into something that was gradually taking over my life. The only way to stop it was to expose it. God knew that, and He graciously worked with me through His Holy Spirit to do so. He brought the right people, books, and other resources into my life to help me realize I was not alone in my pain. Thousands of people had experienced abuse at the hands of parents and other relatives or acquaintances.

The Bible teaches us to confess our faults to one another so we may be healed and learn to love one another (see James 5:16). My father's abusing me was not a fault in me, but I saw it as one. It had to be dealt with and exposed in order for me to be an emotionally, mentally, spiritually, and physically healthy individual.

Everyone needs someone to talk to, someone they feel they can be honest with, someone who won't tell their secrets. If you have trouble accepting yourself, pray and ask God to provide spiritually mature people to be your friends, people you can trust who will listen and understand, but who will also speak God's truth into your life. Also remember that you already have the best friend you will ever have and that is Jesus. You can talk to Him about anything at any time, and He will always listen and understand.

Live Light and Free

When people begin being honest with God, sharing with trustworthy people, studying God's Word, and learning how to live in the light and not be afraid of it, their lives change for the better. God knows everything, and He loves you and me anyway, so even if we never find anyone else to talk to, we can be totally open and honest with Him.

God sees straight through pretense, so just be honest when you talk to Him. Ask Him to reveal to you anything you may be afraid to face—and then buckle your seat belt. You may be in for the ride of your life. It may be bumpy at some times and frightening at others. But one thing is for sure: it is a ride that will eventually take you where you want to go—to a life you can enjoy, one that bears good fruit for God.

Don't be afraid of your weaknesses any longer. Don't allow them to make you hate yourself. Give them all to God, and He will surprise you by using them. Give Him all that you are and especially all that you are not. When you do surrender to God in this way, you will experience a release from the things that burden you. You will be able to live light and free rather than weighed down with burdens.

Don't let your weaknesses and imperfections embarrass you. Give yourself permission to be human, because that's what you are. Love yourself in spite of everything you see wrong with yourself. We all have to deal with our little loads of faults and imperfections. Yours may not be the same as someone else's, but believe me, they are no worse. You are going to have them anyway, so you may as well give yourself permission to be imperfect. Accept it—you are not perfect and never will be. So if you are ever going to approve of yourself, you will have to do it in your imperfect state. God is looking at your heart. If you have your faith in Him and a heart that wants to do right, that is all you need. You are loved and accepted, and you no longer have to live with the agony of an approval addiction. Like the apostle Paul, we should keep pressing toward the mark of perfection, always letting go of past mistakes, and never believing that God rejects us due to our imperfections.

CHAPTER
10

You Don't Have to Live with Approval Addiction

When we think of addictions, we may immediately think of drugs or alcohol. But people can be addicted to almost anything. An addiction is something people feel they cannot live without or something they feel compelled to do in order to relieve pressure, pain, or discomfort of some kind. Drug addicts, for example, do whatever is necessary to get another fix whenever they begin to feel uncomfortable. Alcoholics feel compelled to drink, especially when confronted with life's problems. The substances to which people are addicted help relieve their pain momentarily, but they also perpetuate destructive, controlling cycles in their lives.

We Can't Please Everyone All the Time

We become addicted to approval when we base our self-worth on how people treat us or on what we believe they think about us. The truth is, we do not need certain people to approve of us in order to feel good about ourselves. When we think we do need their approval, we have developed a false belief. We may spend a lot of time and effort trying to please people and gain their approval. But if it takes only one glance of disapproval or one unappreciative word to ruin our sense of self-worth, we are in bondage. No matter how hard we work to please people and gain their acceptance, someone somewhere will always disapprove of us.

Anyone who intends to do much in life must accept the fact that there will be times when everyone around us will not approve of us. I deal with and minister to a wide variety of people; there is no way humanly possible that I can please all of them all the time. At Joyce Meyer Ministries, we have several hundred employees, and we almost never make a decision that pleases all of them. I have had to learn to accept that some people will disapprove of me or of things I do and to rest in the fact that God approves of me.

The Bible says Jesus "made Himself of no reputation" (see Philippians 2:7, NKJV). That is a significant statement. He was not well thought of by many people, but His heavenly Father approved of Him and what He was doing, and that was all that really mattered to Him.

As long as you and I have God's approval, we have what we need most. The apostle Paul said that had he been trying to be popular with people, he would not have been a servant of the Lord Jesus Christ (see Galatians 1:10). Needing people's approval in an unbalanced way can steal our destiny. We cannot always please people if we want to please God, but He will give us favor with the people with whom He truly desires us to be in relationship.

Divine Favor

When we seek to please God and choose to live by faith, He will give us favor with people if we ask and trust Him to do so. Scripture tells us: "When a man's ways please the Lord, He makes even his enemies to be at peace with him" (Proverbs 16:7).

When I first began preaching, I wanted people to like and accept me, of course. I still do. In the beginning of my ministry I did not know much about trusting God for His supernatural favor, so I felt a lot of pressure to do all the "right" things, hoping people would accept me and approve of me.

The problem with that type of mind-set is that everyone expects something different, and no matter how hard we try, we cannot please all of the people all the time. Some people felt my conferences were too long, while others wanted me to spend even more time teaching. Some thought the music was too loud, while others wanted it louder. Most of the people loved my preaching style, but occasionally someone found my straightforward approach offensive and sent me a letter trying to correct me! Disapproval of any kind almost made me sick, literally. I worried about it and struggled with feelings of rejection until I learned to trust God rather than trying to earn acceptance.

In my earlier years, before I allowed God to do a work in me, I did a lot of pretending. Whatever I thought people wanted me to be, I tried to be. I wore many masks, trying to gain everyone's acceptance. This type of behavior can become a real problem if we do not address it and change it. God will never help us be anyone but ourselves.

I had tried to please so many people in so many ways that I cried out to God in frustration one day, "I don't know who I am or how I am supposed to act." At times I felt like a vending machine. Everyone around me pushed a different button, expecting a different result. My husband wanted a good, adoring, submissive wife. My children wanted an attentive mother. My parents and aunt, who are elderly and dependent on me, wanted my attention. The call of God on my life also demanded much from me. The people to whom I ministered wanted me to be available for them whenever they felt they needed me. I said yes to everything until I finally became sick from stress and realized I was headed for serious health issues if I did not learn to say no. I wanted everyone to love me and accept me, I desperately wanted their approval, but I kept trying to get it in the wrong ways.

The Lord told me that He would give me favor with people if I would pray and trust Him. God can cause people who would normally despise us to accept and like us. The Bible says He changes the hearts of men the way He changes the watercourses (see Proverbs 21:1). If God can make a river flow in a specific direction, surely He can change someone's heart toward us. We wear ourselves out trying to do what only God can do.

God can and will open the right doors for you and give you favor with the right people at the right time. For example, God can get you a job far better than anything you could ever get for yourself. Actually, God got me a job I was not even qualified to do and then enabled me to do it. I worked in a business as a general manager and handled things for which most people would need a college degree and many years of experience. At the time I had neither, but God was on my side. We can have favor with God, and He will give us favor with people.

I like to say, "God begins where we end." Stop struggling, trying to make things happen according to your desires, and ask God to take the driver's seat in your life. As long as we try to make things happen by the works of our flesh, God will stand back and wait for us to wear ourselves out. Eventually we will do just that, and hopefully, when we do, we will call upon the Lord.

Pray for favor. Confess that you have favor with God and that He gives you favor with people. James 4:2 says, "You do not have because you do not ask." Start asking for favor regularly, and you will be amazed at the acceptance and blessings that come your way. You will have so many friends you will have to pray about which invitations to take or decline.

Develop your faith in the area of favor. Live expecting it all the time. Remember, you cannot please all the people all the time, but God can give you favor. Trust Him to choose your friends, to open the right doors, and to close the wrong ones. Ask the Lord for divine connections, friendships that will be perfect for you. God can connect you with people who will add to your life rather than take away from it. When He does bring the right relationships into your life, realize that you will need to handle them wisely, and that may include establishing and enforcing good boundaries.

Establish Good Boundaries

People who are addicted to approval frequently get burned out because they continually run the risk of trying to do too much. They so desperately want to please others that they do everything they feel is expected of them and then some. Sometimes they say yes just because they cannot say no, they don't want to disappoint people, or because they may simply be too committed to being nice. They burn out for lack of discernment or because of unwarranted guilt. At the same time, their anger builds.

Burnout makes us angry because we recognize deep down inside that being drained and exhausted is not normal. We become angry with the people pressuring us, when in reality we allow ourselves to be pressured. To avoid pressure from others and from ourselves, we must take control of our lives under the guidance of the Holy Spirit and we must learn to establish healthy boundaries.

Once when I was complaining about my heavy schedule,

I heard the Holy Spirit say, "Joyce, you are the one who makes your schedule. If you don't like it, then do something about it."

We frequently complain and live silently angry lives while at the same time continuing to do the very things that make us angry. It is true that people should not pressure us, but it is equally true that we should not allow ourselves to give in to the pressure they put on us. We cannot blame others or the enemy for things that are ultimately our own responsibilities.

Normal Christian life should take place within the boundaries of balanced living. Even Jesus rested. He walked away from the demands of the crowd and took time for renewal, and we need to do the same.

Boundaries in Relationships

The area of relationships is one in which most people desperately need to be balanced and to maintain healthy boundaries. We must learn to say no and not fear the loss of friendships or other relationships. I have decided that if I lose a relationship because I tell someone no, then I really have no genuine relationship at all with that person.

God desires for us to have enjoyable, healthy relationships. A relationship is not healthy if one person is in control while the other struggles for approval. Nor is it healthy to gain a relationship by being ready to do anything another person wants, no matter what it is or how we feel about it personally. If we have to sin against our own consciences to have someone's approval, we are not following God's will.

You can gain or buy friends by letting them control you, but you will have to keep them the same way you got them. After allowing them to control you to keep their friendship for a while, you will eventually get tired of having no freedom. Being lonely is actually better than being manipulated and controlled.

When you enter into a new relationship, be careful how you get started. What you allow in the beginning will come to be expected throughout your association with that person. The behavior you tolerate at the start of a relationship should be behavior you can be happy with permanently. Let people know by your actions that even though you would like their approval, you can live without it. Respect others, and let them know you expect them to respect you, too.

Sometimes Confrontation Is Necessary

Gaining the respect of others and maintaining healthy relationships with them occasionally requires confrontation. That means you must say no when the other party wants to hear yes. It means you may have to choose to do something you know the other party won't approve of, if you know it is the right choice for you.

If you have not been accustomed to confronting people

and now find yourself controlled and manipulated, making a change may not be easy. Once you develop a pattern of pleasing people, you will need to take a genuine step of faith to break that cycle. Give people their freedom, but stand up for your right to be free as well.

If people are not used to being confronted, they may react aggressively until they get acclimated to the change in your behavior. You may need to explain that you have allowed them to have their way in the past, but that you have been wrong. Explain that you have been insecure and have needed their approval before, but now you have to make a change for your own good. It will be hard for you and for them, but in order to have a healthy relationship, you must do it. If the relationship is a good one, then it will survive the transition. As a matter of fact, going through difficult things and not giving up usually makes a relationship better than it was previously.

Spend some time praying about any confrontation before you enter into it. Ask God to give you courage and to help the other person be willing to understand and receive what you need to say. Never confront anyone without being prepared to also receive correction from them regarding anything you might be doing. Even though it may be difficult for both of you, remember that what is impossible with man is possible with God (see Mark 10:27).

Make a decision right now that with God's help you will break the cycle of approval addiction. Initially, you may feel uncomfortable with the thought that someone is unhappy with you, but remember: your only other choice is spending your life being unhappy. Breaking any addiction produces suffering for a season, but it leads to victory for a lifetime. We can suffer in a never-ending cycle of addiction, or we can suffer on our way to a breakthrough. Your feelings may try to persuade you to go back to your old ways of relating to people, but don't let them win. Keep moving forward!

CHAPTER

12

Don't Let Your Feelings Stop You

Abuse, rejection, abandonment, betrayal, disappointment, judgment, criticism, and other similar situations all cause pain in our lives. Guilt and shame can cause us to withdraw from others and suffer the pain of loneliness. Anger and unforgiveness can fester inside of us like infected wounds.

Emotional pain is often more devastating than physical pain. A pain pill or other medication may alleviate physical pain, but emotional pain is not as easy to deal with. We can be physically sick and everyone feels sorry for us, but if we have emotional problems others may view us suspiciously. But the truth is, our emotions are part of our makeup, and they can wear out or become sick like any other part of the anatomy.

If you have an emotional wound in your life, Jesus wants to heal you. Don't make the mistake of thinking He is only interested in your spiritual life. Jesus can heal you everywhere you hurt! The root cause of an approval addiction is usually an emotional wound. Jesus came to heal our wounds and to bind up and heal our broken hearts, to give us beauty for ashes and the oil of joy to replace our mourning (see Isaiah 61:1–3).

Choose to Choose Right

Even when we hurt, the way to move toward healing is to start making right choices, which can be difficult and painful. Since that is the case, some people never break free from their pain or addictions. On the journey to healing, we often have to do the right thing for a long time before we begin getting right results. We must do right and keep doing right, pressing past how we feel about it. For example, it is emotionally and mentally painful to treat someone right when that person has hurt us in the past. It seems downright unfair or even unwise. After all, why should we be good to someone who has hurt us? Well, if we cannot find any other reason, we can choose to do it just because Jesus instructed us to do so (see Matthew 5:38–44).

If someone has hurt me, and I am bitter about it, that person is actually still hurting me. Bitterness is a pain in itself; it is a negative attitude that steals joy and peace. However, if I am willing to press past the pain and make a decision to forgive, I will be free.

If my husband, Dave, hurts my feelings or disappoints me in some way, it is painful. As long as I refuse to forgive him, the pain remains. As soon as I choose to do as the Bible teaches, which is to forgive and treat him as though nothing happened, I am free (see Matthew 6:14–15). To find freedom from the pain, I have to press past it; I have to choose to do the right thing *while* I am still hurting.

Doing the right thing while we are hurting may mean choosing to forgive someone after they have hurt you terribly, choosing to believe God's Word when your circumstances are extremely difficult, telling the truth when being honest is not easy, being kind to someone who has rejected you in the past, or praying for someone who has used or betrayed you. A variety of situations present us with opportunities to make right choices when it is painful. We may suffer emotionally, but we need to move forward with right decisions anyway and discipline ourselves to stick with them.

It Takes Discipline

The Bible says no discipline for the present seems joyous; nevertheless, later on it will yield the peaceful "fruit of righteousness to those who are trained by it" (see Hebrews 12:11). Righteousness, or doing what is right, is a fruit that brings peace to our lives. Nothing feels better than simply knowing we did what was right.

When confronted with pain, we have three choices: (1) press past the pain now, (2) press past the pain later, or (3) keep the pain forever.

The Bible says discipline is sometimes painful. The very word *discipline* means we will have to do something we don't really feel like doing. If we feel like doing something, we don't need discipline!

I don't have to discipline myself to shop for new clothes, because I like to go shopping. However, I know a woman who hates to shop, and she waits until everything she has is outdated and totally worn out before she will buy something new. She has to discipline herself to shop, because her feelings make her not want to do so. My feelings support me greatly concerning shopping; therefore, I need no discipline to get to my favorite stores. I must discipline myself *not* to shop at times!

We must press past our lack of desire to do things we don't enjoy. In the same way, we must also press past the emotional pain of abuse, rejection, disapproval, betrayal, judgment, guilt, shame, anger, unforgiveness, and criticism in order to be set free from them.

Don't allow your past to ruin your future. God shows us in His Word how we can be free, but we still have to make choices that may not always be easy or even seem fair. Doing so can be difficult, but once you do what you need to do, you will find blessing and reward.

You're Not Alone

We all get hurt at times, and we can choose to let the hurt make us bitter or to let it make us better. How can injustices make us better? For one thing, they help us develop character. Doing what is right when our feelings don't support those actions builds strong character in us.

Not only does everyone get hurt, we all get hurt again and again. That may not sound very encouraging, but it is true. Our efforts to avoid being hurt often keep us from developing real relationships with people. We should not spend all of our time trying to protect ourselves. We should be willing to give ourselves away and to lay down our lives for others (see John 15:13).

The Bible reminds us in 1 Peter 5:9 that we are to stand firm in faith against the attacks of the devil, knowing that identical sufferings are appointed to our brothers and sisters throughout the world. We may think other people never have to go through anything difficult, but we all go through different situations. Some people have suffered devastating situations that no one else knows anything about. They go to God with their problems instead of telling others about them. Some people have learned the art of suffering silently. They know only God can help them, so they don't bother telling everyone they meet what they are going through.

Sharing our troubles with a friend or counselor is not wrong, but we cannot assume others have no challenges in life just because they don't look depressed or don't talk about their problems.

My husband rarely talks about anything he is going through. At times I have had a virus of some sort and told

Dave my symptoms. Occasionally he has replied, "I had that a couple of weeks ago. I felt really bad for seven days."

When I asked him why he didn't tell me he was sick, he replied, "Why should I tell you how bad I feel? You can't do anything for me."

Some people are talkers and some are not. Don't make the mistake of thinking people have no pain just because they have not told you about it. I believe it is important for us not to think we are the only ones hurting (see 1 Peter 5:9). Remembering this truth keeps us from feeling alone and isolated in our pain. When we are hurting, it helps to remember that we are not alone, and with God's help we will make it through our difficulties and receive God's reward.

Isaiah 61:7–8 says:

Instead of your [former] shame you shall have a two-fold recompense; instead of dishonor and reproach [your people] shall rejoice in their portion. Therefore in their land they shall possess double [what they had forfeited]; everlasting joy shall be theirs. For I the Lord love justice.

The promise of reward helps us press past the pain of disciplining ourselves to be obedient.

CHAPTER
13

Press Past the Pain of Disapproval

A specific pain that people must press through when breaking free from approval addiction is the pain of disapproval. Those who are addicted to approval feel emotional and mental pain when they experience disapproval. Approval addicts attempt to avoid or relieve the pain of disapproval by doing whatever people want them to do.

A young woman I'll call Jenny is addicted to approval. Her mother has always been difficult to please and is very controlling; Jenny has felt the pain of rejection many times in her life. Like any child, she has the completely normal desire of wanting her mother's approval.

Jenny has fallen into the trap of people pleasing in her relationship with her mother. Her mother expects Jenny to drop what she is doing to cater to her every whim. She becomes angry if Jenny has already made plans and is unable to accommodate her. Jenny's mother is unreasonable, but Jenny's approval addiction feeds her mother's addiction to control.

In order to be able to enjoy her life and her mother, Jenny will have to choose to do what is right for herself, even if her mother will disapprove. She must also be willing to endure the pain of rejection.

The decision not to give in to her mother's desires will be hard for Jenny emotionally, because she has always let her mother have her way. The new relational dynamics won't be easy for Jenny's mother, either, because she is addicted to getting what she wants. She needs to be in control in order to feel good about herself.

Do you see the trap Satan sets for people? Jenny needs approval, and her mother needs to be in control. Her mother's problem controls Jenny, and Jenny's problem in turn feeds her mother's. Each time Jenny says no to her mother and sticks with her decision, the discomfort she feels will lessen.

The same principle applies to any area of life that needs discipline. We want anything we are accustomed to having. If we don't get it, we feel discomfort until we get used to doing without it. We can starve an addiction to death by simply not feeding it. We don't have to fight with an addiction; we can simply draw strength from God and refuse to feed it.

Jenny will have to endure some difficulty for a period of time. At times the difficulty will seem to be more than she can stand, but if she refuses to go back to allowing her mother to control her, eventually she will be free, and Jenny and her mother will be able to begin developing a new and healthy relationship. If they are both willing, Jenny and her mother can indeed start afresh.

The Only Worthy Addiction

I mentioned that Jenny may go through times when she feels her pain and discomfort are more than she can stand. What is she to do during those times? She needs to run quickly to the Lord—to His Word and His promises. If she will study those portions of Scripture that strengthen and encourage her, they will enable her to keep her commitment to break free and to do the right thing.

God's Word has inherent power in it. When we release our faith in His Word, that power is released into our lives and circumstances to help us. I want to encourage you to replace one addiction with another. Actually, I want you to replace all addictions with one other addiction: I want you to become addicted to Jesus and to the Word of God! They are what you need more than anything else.

Determination and discipline are important in breaking the cycle of addictions, but receiving supernatural strength from God is the key to real success. Learn to run to Him instead of running to the substance or the wrong behavior to which you are addicted. Every unhealthy addiction can be broken in your life. You can live a balanced, joy-filled, peaceful life if you will lean on

God in everything and for everything. His grace (divine favor and enabling power) is sufficient to meet all of our needs.

Set Your Mind and Keep It Set

God wants to be everything to us, and the Bible says we are to set our minds and keep them set on things above, not on earthly things (see Colossians 3:2). Having been addicted to approval, I know how difficult it is not to think about a situation when we feel someone is not pleased with us. Thoughts of that person's anger and rejection seem to fill every moment.

Instead of trying not to think wrong thoughts, choose right ones. Fill your mind with positive thoughts. Meditate on God's Word and His will for you. Then the wrong thoughts will not be able to gain access to your mind.

We must be armed with right thinking or we will give up during hard times. Realize that moving from being a victim to being a victor will not be a quick process. Breaking free from approval addiction will take time, but the investment will be worth it. Remember, you can either go through the temporary pain of deliverance or keep the pain of bondage that never ends until it is confronted.

Confront Rejection

As you break the approval addiction, you may face fears of rejection, of abandonment, of being alone, and of what people will think or say about you. Fear is not from God: "For God did not give us a spirit of timidity (of cowardice, of craven and cringing and fawning fear), but [He has given us a spirit] of power and of love and of calm and well-balanced mind and discipline and self-control" (2 Timothy 1:7).

The idea of fear conveys fleeing or running away from something. God does not want us to run from things. He wants us to confront things, knowing that He has promised to be with us, to never leave us nor forsake us (see Hebrews 13:5).

There are times when we must do things even when afraid. In other words, we must do what we know we should do even though we feel fear. When God says in His Word, "fear not," He means for us to keep going forward, taking steps of obedience to carry out His instructions. He is in essence saying, "This is not going to be easy, but don't run away from it."

Approval addicts are especially afraid of the pain of rejection. They will spend their lives keeping other people happy and "fixed" while forfeiting their own joy, unless they choose to break the cycle of addiction. They will have to "do it afraid." They will have to follow the leading of the Holy Spirit and their own hearts rather than follow other people's desires and opinions.

The only way out is through!

Press Past the Fear of Loneliness

As part of breaking approval addiction, we may not only fear that people will reject us, we may also be afraid of being lonely. We must press past the pain of being lonely and feeling misunderstood. We must trust God for right relationships and not make emotional decisions that only end up making our problems worse. The fear of being lonely can turn us into people pleasers, and we can end up with no life of our own, feeling used and bitter.

Some people isolate themselves out of the fear of rejection. They think they cannot get hurt if they don't get involved with others, but the result is that they are lonely. Other people are afraid to trust. They fear being honest and vulnerable, afraid that people will judge and criticize them or tell their secrets if they share anything private or personal. All these fears only add to the feelings of loneliness that many people experience.

Press past your pain all the way to victory. Be determined! Stop just wishing things were different and do your part to make them different. There are two types of people in the world: those who wait for something to happen and those who make something happen. We cannot do anything apart from God, but we can decide to cooper-

ate with Him. We can face the truth. We can stop feeding our addictions and endure the pain of letting them die
from lack of nourishment.

It is time for a change! Get excited about your future
and realize that when you are going through something,
the good news is that you are going *through*—and that
means you will ultimately come out the other side with a
victory that cannot be taken away from you.

PART 3

Putting an End to People Pleasing

CHAPTER
14

Who Do You Want to Please?

We are to be God pleasers, not self pleasers or people pleasers. Most approval addicts are also people pleasers. We usually discover as we go through life that if we don't please people, they don't approve of us. If we also have an unbalanced need for approval, we have no choice but to become people pleasers.

The apostle Paul said that he did not seek popularity with man: "Now am I trying to win the favor of men, or of God? Do I seek to please men? If I were still seeking popularity with men, I should not be a bond servant of Christ (the Messiah)" (Galatians 1:10). Yet he also stated that he tried to please people and accommodate their opinions and desires so they might be saved:

Just as I myself strive to please [to accommodate myself to the opinions, desires, and interests of others, adapting myself to] all men in everything I do, not aiming at or considering my own profit and advantage, but that of many in order that they may be saved.

—1 Corinthians 10:33

When we consider these two verses, they almost seem contradictory, but if we understand the heart behind them we will see that they don't disagree at all.

Paul wanted to please people. He wanted to maintain good relationships with others, especially for the purpose of leading them to accept Jesus as their Savior. He also wanted to please God and fulfill God's call on his life. Paul knew how to maintain balance in this area. He tried to please people, as long as pleasing them did not cause him to displease the Lord. He wrote in Acts 5:29, "We must obey God rather than men."

Pleasing people is good, but becoming a people pleaser is not. I define *people pleasers* as those who try to please people even if they have to compromise their consciences to do so. People pleasers need approval so desperately that they allow others to control, manipulate, and use them. They let their emotions dictate their behavior instead of allowing the Holy Spirit to lead them. People pleasers are fear-based individuals, and their motives are almost entirely rooted in fear. They fear rejection, judgment, what people think and say, and especially anger or disapproval.

The "Why" behind the "What"

Our reasons for doing the things we do—our motives—are very important. God wants us to have pure hearts. He wants us to do what we do because we believe He is leading us or because it is the right thing to do. God wants love to be our motive in all things. We should do what we do for the love of God and others. Being motivated by fear instead of love or faith does not please God.

We should regularly ask ourselves why we do what we do. Our actions and behaviors do not impress God; He looks at the *why* behind *what* we do. God instructs us in His Word not to do good deeds to be seen. We are not to do things to be recognized and honored.

Every deed that *appears* to be good is not necessarily good; a work is good only if it is done in the will of God, meaning with a pure motive. Two people can do the same good deed, yet God may not consider it good for both of them. One person may be in the will of God, and the other may be outside His will, depending on each one's motives for his actions.

I strive to do what I do with the right motives. If I am invited to a function, and I really don't feel God is leading me to go, or if I know my schedule cannot accommodate it without becoming stressful, I don't go! When people want to hear yes, and you tell them no, they don't like it. But true friends will give you the freedom to make your own decisions and then respect the decisions you make.

They will not pressure you or try to make you feel guilty for not pleasing them. Your real friends don't use you for their own benefit or become angry when you don't do what they want you to do.

We must not blame others if we are afraid of them or of the ways they respond to us. Fearing people more than we fear God is offensive to Him. We should not fear God in the wrong ways, but we should have a respectful fear of Him, knowing that He means what He says. Since God has told us in His Word that we are not to be people pleasers, we should take that directive seriously and not allow out-of-balance, people-pleasing attitudes in our lives.

Your opinion of yourself is more important than other people's opinions of you. You cannot feel good about yourself if you know your actions do not have God's approval. It is not good if you say yes and then disrespect yourself because you cannot say no. Live to please God and learn to respect yourself.

Be Honest

One thing that definitely pleases God and will help you respect yourself is to be honest. Be honest with yourself and be honest with others. This means saying yes when you need to say yes and no when you need to say no. The Bible says we are to be truthful in all things; we are to speak the truth, love the truth, and walk in the truth.

Ephesians 4:15 says, "Let our lives lovingly express

truth [in all things, speaking truly, dealing truly, living truly]." But approval addicts often tell lies because they fear people won't accept the truth. They say yes with their mouths while their hearts are screaming no. They may not want to do something, but they act as though they do, because they are afraid of displeasing someone. If they ever do say no, they usually make an excuse for why they cannot do what is being asked of them. They may not feel it is the right thing for them to do, or they may not feel peaceful about doing it.

If we would just be bold enough to speak the truth, we could save ourselves a lot of time and trouble. We don't want to be rude, but neither do we want to be liars. Most people pleasers are not honest about their desires, feelings, and thoughts. They tell people what they want to hear, not what they need to hear. A healthy relationship demands honesty. Some people may not want to hear the truth, but that does not relieve us of the responsibility to speak the truth.

Be obedient to God and be honest with yourself and with others, no matter what people think or say. Live to please Him, not the people around you. If people around you are pleased with your words and actions, that is good; but make it your goal to please God above all.

CHAPTER
15

What Do You Need?

People pleasers and approval addicts quickly and regularly set aside their own legitimate needs. Denying those needs eventually builds into an explosive situation. Constantly trying to please others is draining, which is why many people pleasers feel anxious, worried, unhappy, and tired much of the time. They resent the fact that other people don't do much for them, but instead of meeting their own legitimate needs in healthy, appropriate ways, they often deny the fact that they have those needs.

People pleasers may think asking for help will make others feel obligated to them. Although they do most of what they do out of a sense of obligation, they don't want others to feel obligated to them. Most people pleasers have such a poor self-image that they believe people would not want to do anything for them, anyway. They don't value themselves, so they think no one else values them, either.

Many people pleasers were raised in homes in which

their needs and feelings were not valued, respected, or considered important. As children, they were expected to respond to or take care of other people's needs. This is why most people pleasers focus primarily on others and away from themselves. Sometimes they don't know what they feel or think, or even what they want for themselves. They are so good at denying their needs that they don't even ask themselves if they have any.

Someone I'll call Patty was raised in a dysfunctional home. Patty's father was an alcoholic, and he was verbally abusive. As a result, she learned to totally disregard her needs and to spend her time taking care of others. She developed a martyr complex. She did things for people but resented doing so. Patty felt taken advantage of, but she would not accept anything for herself even when it was offered, because she did not feel she was worth anything.

Patty lived under tremendous stress, most of which she placed on herself because of the way she was raised. As an adult, she was diagnosed with severe arthritis that caused her great pain. The combination of her emotional and physical pain was more than she could handle. She became very depressed.

Patty began going to a counselor who asked her what she wanted out of life. She could not tell him because she had never even thought about what *she* wanted. She had to learn that having needs and desires was not wrong. She had been so accustomed to not getting anything she wanted that she simply did not bother wanting anything at all. She was afraid to desire anything because she felt she had no right to do so. She felt worthless and devalued.

Watching Patty begin to recognize and accept her legitimate needs and to expect people to meet them was very refreshing to those around her. She began to have hopes and dreams for her life, which gave her something to look forward to. She is now well on her way to breaking free from her people-pleasing addiction.

We all have needs, especially emotional needs such as love, encouragement, and companionship—someone to connect with and confide in. We also need acceptance, approval, and enjoyment.

We Need Enjoyment

When I was growing up, I did not enjoy myself. I was never really allowed to act like a child. I can remember getting into trouble and being corrected for playing. Our house was not enjoyable; it was filled with fear.

As an adult Christian, I realized I felt guilty if I attempted to enjoy myself. I felt safe if I was working, but enjoyment was something I denied myself. I did not feel it was a legitimate need for me. I resented other people who did not work as long and hard as I did. My husband really enjoyed his life and that made me angry, because I felt he could accomplish so much more in life if he would be more serious.

I realize now that I was not angry because Dave enjoyed

his life; I was angry because I did not enjoy mine. But I was the only one who could do anything about it. Resenting Dave and others was foolish, because the enjoyment they found in life was also available to me for the taking.

The Holy Spirit worked with me a long time before I finally understood that God wanted me to enjoy my life. Jesus actually said, "I came that you might have and enjoy your life" (see John 10:10). We need enjoyment. Without it, life is unbalanced, and we open a door for the enemy to devour us (see 1 Peter 5:8).

Make sure you are not denying your legitimate needs. Helping others is part of our call as Christians, but doing things for ourselves is not wrong! Be sure you take time for yourself. Be determined to enjoy your life and take time to do so. You only go around once, so be sure you enjoy the ride!

We Need Boundaries

One way we ensure our ability to enjoy life is to have boundaries. Just as a person puts up a fence around his property to keep intruders out, so you must establish your personal limits and margins—invisible lines you draw in your life to protect yourself from being used and abused. If you had a privacy fence around your yard, and on a sunny afternoon you looked out and saw your neighbors sunbathing in your yard while their children played without permission, what would you do? You would not simply say, "Oh, my, I do wish those neighbors would leave me alone." You would probably be very forceful in letting them know that your yard is off-limits to them for such activities without your permission.

You need to be just as forceful in letting people know you expect them to respect the limits and margins you have established around your personal life. If you don't want friends showing up at your house without calling ahead of time and getting your approval, don't just let them do it and then resent them for it. Enforce your guidelines even if you end up losing your friends, because real friends respect your boundaries.

As I have mentioned, allowing others to take advantage of you is your fault, not theirs. Be aware of what you need, and don't let others convince you that you don't have needs or aren't worth having your needs met. Begin now to enjoy your life and to establish boundaries that will keep you healthy and happy for years to come.

CHAPTER
16

Take Authority over Your Life

People pleasers and approval addicts do not live within limits or margins. In their efforts to please people, they push themselves beyond reasonable boundaries. Let's face it: people often expect us to do things we either should not or cannot do.

Being a people pleaser is painful. Some people pleasers rarely focus on themselves properly. When they do take a moment for themselves, they feel selfish, indulgent, and guilty; this is why they are often on the go, rushing to get things done, striving to keep everyone happy. Because they stay so busy doing for others, they usually work harder than most people. Because they accomplish so much more than others and are so easy to get along with, they are often first to be asked to do certain things. As a result, they are vulnerable to being taken advantage of, because they usually don't even consider that saying no is an option for them. They simply assume they should do whatever anyone asks them to do, no matter how unreasonable it is. When they do venture out and say no to a request, they often change that no to a yes if people act angry or displeased.

People pleasers will push beyond the bounds of reason if they think doing so means everyone will be happy with them. We need to understand this basic fact of human nature: most people will take advantage of us if we let them. We cannot depend on others to treat us fairly and honestly. Often we become bitter and resentful toward those who do take advantage of us, not realizing that we are just as guilty as they are, if not more so.

I once had an employer who took advantage of me. He required me to work so many hours that I was not able to spend proper time with my family. I was worn out and never had time for myself. He never showed appreciation, and no matter what I did he always expected more. If I even mildly indicated that I might not be able to comply with one of his requests, his anger would start to surface. When that happened, I caved in and agreed to do what he asked of me.

As the years passed I resented his control more and more. As I was praying about the situation one day and moaning to God about how unfair it was, He said, "What your boss is doing is wrong, but not confronting it is just as wrong." This was hard for me to hear. Like most people I wanted to blame someone else for my lack of courage. Had I not been a people pleaser and had I not been afraid of my boss, I would have saved myself about five years of being so stressed that I eventually got very sick. My boss wasn't my problem; *I* was my problem. As I said earlier, many people will take advantage of us if we allow it. I allowed him to take advantage of me.

God has given you authority first and foremost over your own life. If you don't accept and exercise that authority, you may spend your life blaming others for things you should do something about. Make your own decisions according to what you believe is God's will for you; don't let others make your decisions for you. On Judgment Day, God will not ask anyone else to give an account of your life; He will ask only you (see Romans 14:12).

Learn to Ask for Help and to Delegate

Although people pleasers often struggle to do so, setting proper limits and margins is extremely wise. Doing so is a sign of strength, not weakness. Asking for help is also a good thing to do. God has placed certain people in each of our lives to help us. If we do not receive their help, we become frustrated and overworked, and they feel unfulfilled because they are not using their gifts. Remember that God has not called you to do everything for everybody in every situation. You cannot be all things to all people all the time. You have legitimate needs. It is not wrong to need help and ask for it. However, needing help and being too proud to ask for it is wrong.

In Exodus 18:12–27, we see that Moses had many responsibilities. The people looked to him for everything, and he tried to meet all their needs. His father-in-law saw the situation and said to Moses, "What is this that you do for the people? Why do you sit alone, and all the people stand around you from morning till evening?" (v. 14).

Moses proceeded to tell his father-in-law how all the people came to him with their questions. They wanted him to sit as judge between them. The people wanted Moses to meet their needs, and he wanted to please them.

Moses' father-in-law told him that spending so much time and energy being involved in people's circumstances was not good. He suggested that Moses delegate some of his authority to others. He said Moses should let them make the minor decisions and deal only with the difficult situations himself. Moses took his father-in-law's advice, and it enabled him to endure the strain of his task. At the same time, the people gained a sense of accomplishment for the decisions they made on their own.

Many people either complain frequently about what they are expected to do or end up falling apart emotionally and physically because they won't let anyone help them do anything. They don't think anyone is as qualified for the job as they are.

Learn to delegate. Let as many people help you as possible. If you do, you will have a lot more energy and stamina in the long run and enjoy yourself a lot more.

PART 4

Finding Freedom from Comparison, Rejection, and Control

CHAPTER
17

Really, It's Okay

People pleasers and approval addicts feel awful when their decisions do not please others. They assume responsibility for other people's emotional reactions. In my former life, if I thought someone was angry, unhappy, or disappointed, I was uncomfortable, and I could not feel comfortable again until I tried my hardest to make that person happy.

I did not realize that as long as I was following God's will for my life, other people's responses were not my responsibility. It may not always be possible to do what other people want, but a spiritually mature person learns to deal with disappointment and keep a good attitude. If you are doing what you believe God has told you to do and others are not pleased with you, it is not your fault; it's theirs.

When I was growing up, my father was angry most of the time. I spent most of my time playing the peacemaker in the home. I constantly tried to keep him happy because I was afraid of his anger.

When I became an adult, I continued this practice, except I did it with everybody. Anytime I was with anyone who seemed unhappy, I always felt that person's bad mood was probably my fault; and even if it wasn't my fault, I felt I needed to fix it. I did whatever I thought would please people just so they would stay happy, not realizing that their personal happiness was their responsibility, not mine.

If you are not able to give people what they want, and they become unhappy, it is not your fault. Beware of developing a false sense of responsibility. You have enough legitimate responsibilities in life without taking on illegitimate ones.

If you are in authority—and most people have authority over something, even if it is only the cat or the dog—you must realize that you can rarely make decisions that please everyone. If you are addicted to approval, you will make a poor authority figure. But if you can learn to feel good about following God instead of pleasing people, you will become a stronger, better person.

"I Should Be Able to Do More"

Another thing we need to avoid doing is comparing ourselves with others and feeling we should be able to do more than we are doing. Comparison causes us to put a lot of unnecessary pressure on ourselves. If we see that others can do more than we can, or that their endurance is greater than ours, we often feel we should be able to do more. Because we feel guilty, we may push ourselves beyond our reasonable limits and end up sick and unhappy.

We are all different, and we all have different limits. Know yourself, and don't feel bad if you cannot do what someone else can do. A variety of factors, even our God-given temperaments, help determine our limits in various areas.

I know someone named Paula who is married and has three children. She is a full-time mother and homemaker, but unless she has help cleaning her home once a week, she struggles to get everything done and remain peaceful.

Paula has a friend named Mary, who is also married and has five children. Mary works outside the home two days per week and does all her own housework, cooking, and laundry with no extra help. Actually, Mary seems to be more peaceful and less temperamental than Paula, even though she has more to do.

Paula feels bad about herself because she cannot seem to get everything done without help. In her thoughts and conversations, she constantly compares herself to Mary and feels she should be more like her.

Mary's temperament is the easygoing, "cast your care" type. Paula, on the other hand, is very melancholy, a borderline perfectionist who is not comfortable unless everything is in order.

Paula puts herself under so much pressure that she has become difficult to get along with. She carries a burden of guilt most of the time, and it has started affecting her mood and her health. Thankfully, she is now getting help through a book that is teaching her that we are all different, and that is perfectly acceptable. In fact, it is God's design.

We cannot control the temperaments we are born with; they are God's choice. We can work with the Holy Spirit to achieve balance, but basically we are who we are. I will always be a type-A, strong-willed, leadership-type person. In fact, most of the time I am type A+. Dave will always be more easygoing than I am, but that does not mean I should strive to be like he is. I may learn some things from his example, but I still have to be the basic person God created me to be.

Some people do things faster than others, but slower people may do them more neatly. Each of us must do what we are comfortable with. It is not wrong for Paula to need a housekeeper once a week and for Mary not to need one. I am sure that in some other areas, Mary has needs that Paula does not have.

For a long time, Paula felt she should be able to do more because she saw Mary do more, but the fact was that she could not do more and maintain her composure. That was not a weakness in her; it was just the way God put her together. She did not need to be able to do what Mary did in order to approve of herself. She felt Mary was judging her when, in reality, she was judging herself and Mary hadn't thought anything about it. Thankfully, Paula is now beginning to accept herself and to accept Mary without comparing or feeling guilty.

Concern about what people may be thinking or saying about us often controls us. We assume people think certain critical things about us, when the truth is that they are not even thinking about us at all!

When we seek favor and acceptance from our critics, we lose confidence or stray from the path of healthy choices. Stand up to your critics or you will end up being controlled. Do the best you can, be the best "you" that you can be, and do not feel you should be able to do more just because someone else does more. Just be yourself, and don't pressure yourself to perform exactly the way others do. And remember: a strong confidence in God and your own ability to hear from God and being led by the Spirit are the antidote. God has not given and never will give someone else the job of running your life.

CHAPTER
18

Reject Rejection

Many people who are addicted to approval have a great fear of rejection. Jesus taught His disciples in Matthew 10:14 how to handle rejection: "Shake it off." Basically, He said, "Don't let it bother you. Don't let it keep you from doing what I have called you to do."

Jesus was despised and rejected (see Isaiah 53:3), yet He never seemed to let it bother Him. I am sure He felt pain just as you and I do when we experience rejection, but He did not let it keep Him from fulfilling His purpose.

Jesus told His disciples not to be concerned about rejection, because in reality, people who rejected them were really rejecting Him: "He who hears and heeds you [disciples] hears and heeds Me; and he who slights and rejects you slights and rejects Me; and he who slights and rejects Me slights and rejects Him who sent Me" (Luke 10:16).

Rejection is one of Satan's favorite tools to use against people. The pain of rejection often causes people to function in fear rather than boldness. It also results in people pleasing, because those who feel rejected are afraid to say no to others.

The Lord loves His children, and He takes it personally when anyone rejects us or treats us contemptibly. I know from experience and from seeing others who have been rejected that rejection can affect people adversely in serious ways. God wants to set us free from rejection and to build our lives on the firm foundation of His love.

How's Your Foundation?

A person who is rooted in rejection early in life is like a house with a crack in its foundation. The first home Dave and I built had a crack in the basement, and it caused problems periodically for years. Every time storms or heavy rains came, the basement leaked, and everything in the path of the water's flow got wet. We tried three or four different methods before we were finally successful in getting the crack totally repaired.

People who have experienced rejection remind me of that house. Each time a storm or difficult situation arises in their lives, everything becomes a mess, including them. They try different methods to find security, but nothing ever works. They may try people pleasing to find acceptance. Often they become approval addicts. They live with the emotional pain of rejection—or the fear of being rejected, which is often worse than rejection itself.

A solid foundation is the most important part of a building. Without it, the building won't last long. Everything else concerning the building is constructed on the foundation. If the foundation is weak or cracked, nothing built on it is safe. It could crumble or fall apart at any time, especially if something like a storm or an earthquake stresses it.

The Bible encourages us to have a firm foundation in life by building our lives on solid rock, not sand. The person who hears and obeys the Word of God is like the man who, in building his house, dug down deep and laid a foundation upon a rock. When the floodwaters rose, the torrent broke against that house and could not shake it, because it was securely anchored in the rock (see Matthew 7:24–27).

If we try to build our lives on what people say and think of us—how they treat us, how we feel, or our past mistakes—we are building on sinking sand. Even if we have done so, we can build a new foundation for our lives starting now, one that is established on the rock of Jesus Christ and His love. The apostle Paul prayed for the church, that we would be rooted deeply in God's love: "May Christ through your faith [actually] dwell (settle down, abide, make His permanent home) in your hearts! May you be rooted deep in love and founded securely on love" (Ephesians 3:17). You may not have had a good beginning, but you can definitely have a good finish!

The Root of Rejection

When a person's life is built on rejection, that person has a "root" of rejection. The word *root* refers to the starting point of something, the first growth of a seed. Just as bad roots in a plant cannot produce good fruit, a root of rejection cannot lead to a happy, secure life. A root of rejection leads to a faulty foundation for living.

Often, people who are rooted in and built on rejection don't understand why they do the things they do. When people exhibit bad behavior and do not know why, they certainly cannot change it. For many years, when I behaved badly, people asked me, "Why do you act that way? Why do you respond that way?" Their questions frustrated me, because I did not have any answers. I knew my behavior was confusing and unstable, but I didn't know what to do about it. Most of the time I just blamed it on someone else or made excuses.

I responded fearfully to many situations, sometimes in ways that made no sense at all. For example, if Dave pulled into someone's driveway to turn the car around, I became frantic, especially if we had to wait for other cars to pass by behind us before he could complete his turn. I said things like, "You shouldn't turn around in other people's driveways; the home owners won't like it!" Or, "Hurry up and get out of here!"

For a long time I did not understand such reactions, until God showed me that I was reacting to the situation based on how I thought my father would have felt about someone turning around in his driveway; he would have been angry. I was afraid the home owners would come out the front door yelling, as my father would have. The deep-seated fear of rejection in my life caused me to react fearfully to many situations that seem ordinary to an emotionally healthy person.

Are you behaving in any ways that seem confusing to you or to others? Have you ever wondered, *Where did that come from?* or *Why do I act that way?* I hope that realizing that your "fruit" (your actions or behavior) comes from your roots is helpful to you. If you have been rooted in rejection, there is hope. If you feel trapped in behavior you don't understand, do not despair. The Holy Spirit will help you stop reacting to old situations and teach you to act on God's Word. He will give you an entirely new root system, one that will produce good fruit for His kingdom and is totally free from rejection.

John 3:18 states that those who believe in Jesus suffer no judgment, no condemnation, and no rejection. Jesus gives us freely what we struggle to earn from people and never seem to get: freedom from judgment, condemnation, and rejection!

You Will Survive

Start believing you can survive rejection if you need to do so. Jesus was rejected, and He survived. You can, too!

Value the unconditional love of God more than the conditional approval of other human beings, and you will overcome rejection. When I say you will survive and overcome, I don't mean you will just barely make it. I mean that rejection really will not bother you at all. You just need to develop a new attitude toward it.

If you have a problem in this area, stop torturing yourself with concern about what people think. You can survive rejection. You will live through it, and when people are finished thinking unkind thoughts about you, they will go on to think about someone else. You will have the rest of your life to live, and you can live without them. If you have God, you have all you need. If He knows you need anything else, He will provide that too (see Matthew 6:8, 33–34).

You are not responsible for your reputation, anyway. God is! So relax and keep saying to yourself, "I can survive rejection. I am not addicted to approval." Say it over and over until you believe it and are no longer bothered by the way people treat you. When Satan knows he cannot hurt you with rejection, he will stop working through people to bring that type of pain into your life. Then you will begin to see that you have a great future ahead of you!

CHAPTER
19

Break Free from Control

We cannot move freely and confidently into the great future God has planned for us if we don't learn to break the influences that seek to control us. God sent Jesus, His only Son, to purchase our freedom with His life.

If you are letting someone control your life—intimidate you, manipulate you, and cause you to do what you know in your heart is not right—then you need to break those controlling powers. God's will is for us not to be controlled by anyone except His Holy Spirit. God won't force His will on us, so we certainly should not let other people force their desires on us.

Approval addicts almost always end up being controlled and manipulated by other people. It is very unwise to allow others to control you by making your decisions for you. The Bible does say there is safety in many counselors (see Proverbs 11:14). Considering what other wise people say is a good idea, but the final decisions in your life must be yours to make.

God said, "I have set before you life and death, the blessings and the curses; therefore choose life, that you and your descendants may live" (Deuteronomy 30:19). If you are going to choose life, then you must also choose to confront the people who try to control you.

What Control Looks Like

I want to point out that there are two main types of control: emotional control and verbal control.

Emotional Control

Emotional manipulation is one of the most evident and powerful characteristics of control. Tears, rage, and silence (especially silence as a form of rejection) are all methods that controlling people frequently use to manipulate others.

Think about a recently married couple. Perhaps both sets of parents want the newlyweds to spend the holidays with them. Controlling parents may use silence, rage, tears, or anger to get their way. They may remind the couple of "all the money we gave you." This, of course, makes the couple feel indebted, in which case the parents did not really "give" them anything. True giving has no strings attached by which the givers can pull the receivers in whatever direction they want them to go.

In contrast, parents who act properly will allow the couple freedom to make decisions for themselves; they will not pressure them. If they are Christian parents, they will probably pray for God to lead them and their children, and then go on about their business, trusting God to work it out. Parents who apply the least amount of pressure may not always get to spend holidays with their adult children, but they will receive the most love, admiration, and respect from them.

Although I was deceived about the true nature of my actions, I tried emotional manipulation for years. Every time Dave did not do what I wanted him to do, I got angry, went silent, cried, pouted, acted pitiful, and cleaned house or worked hard at other chores hoping to make him feel guilty or sorry for me. It did not work.

No matter how I acted, Dave stayed happy and did what he felt he should do. Had I been successful in controlling him with my emotions, I might still be in the same bondage. He confronted me and refused to allow my behavior to affect him, and I am glad. His lack of confrontation would have enabled me to continue my controlling ways. If you are a controller and want to be brave, pray that God will lead people to confront you anytime you really need it. Then pray that you will receive the confrontation without responding defensively with anger, accusations, or excuses.

Verbal Control

Some people may try to control you with words of failure, defeat, unnatural obligation, guilt, criticism, and intimidation. Sometimes they use threats. For instance, they may threaten you with loss of relationship (rejection). In other words, they may infer that if you don't do what they want you to do, they will no longer want to be in a relationship with you. I believe many teenagers get involved in drugs, alcohol, and sexual misconduct because they are threatened with loss of relationships. We call it "peer pressure," but it's actually control.

How to Recognize a Controller

If you are being controlled, the controller is probably someone you love and respect, or at least someone you liked and respected at one time. You may have lost your respect for the person because of the control, but are so caught up in the cycle that you do not know how to break free.

The controller may be someone you need, and the controller knows it. It may be someone who supports you financially, and you don't know what you would do if that person were not in your life. It could be someone to whom you feel indebted for some reason, someone who has done a lot for you in the past—and who regularly reminds you of it. It could be someone you hurt in the past, and now you feel you need to make up for it for the rest of your life.

The controller may also be someone you are afraid of. You may be afraid of personal harm or loss, as when parents threaten to remove children from a will and not leave them anything if they don't do everything the parents want them to do.

Or the controller may be someone who was controlled in childhood and now functions in learned behavior. It may be a proud, selfish, or lazy person, someone who wants and expects everybody else to serve him.

The controller may also be a deeply insecure or fearful person who feels better about life when he is in control. He may need the number one position to feel safe.

What Kind of People Get Controlled?

The person who is most likely to be controlled is someone who has always been controlled, so being controlled is a habit, a way of life. Such a person is not accustomed to making his own decisions. He may be an insecure, fearful, or timid person who has never practiced confronting anything or anybody. His excuse is "I don't like to confront." My answer is "We all have to do things we don't like to do."

A person who is controlled may be confused about submission to authority. He may not be able to tell the difference between true godly submission and a wrong type of demonically instigated control. He needs to know that the enemy controls; God leads.

A controlled person may have a poor self-image. He may think so little of himself and his abilities that he assumes everyone else is always right and he is always wrong. Anytime anyone disagrees with him, he may instantly shut down inside and submit.

The controlled person may be dependent on others for care, finances, a place to live, employment, companionship, or other things. The controlled person may have done wrong at one time and now feels he owes a debt to the controller, so he allows the control to continue.

Five Steps to Freedom from Control

If you are unable to interact with others without a controller making you feel tense and guilty that you are enjoying yourself, you are being controlled.

Or perhaps you cannot make new friends without the controller becoming jealous or possessive. You feel you always have to check in with the controller before you do anything. You have no personal life. You have to tell the controller everything, invite him everywhere, and get his opinion on everything.

Maybe you have the controller on your mind excessively because you live with a vague fear of what he will think or say about everything you do.

These are signs of a crisis that must be addressed. Let's

take a look at five important steps in gaining freedom from control.

1. The first step to breaking free from control is to recognize you are being controlled. Don't think you are simply keeping the peace by failing to confront wrong behavior.

2. Once you recognize you are being controlled, choose to do something about it. Do not let it continue. This will take some prayer and determination; don't be discouraged if it also takes some time.

3. Learn how the person controls you. Is it through fear, anger, silence, rage, tears, guilt, threats, or some other means? Quickly recognize the control tactics and resist them immediately.

4. You may be afraid to confront, but you must do so even if you have to do it afraid. If you stand firm, the controller will ultimately move from anger to respect. You may fear losing the relationship, and that is a possibility. All I can say is that you would be better off without the relationship than spending your life being controlled and manipulated.

5. Don't try to make any of these changes without a lot of prayer. Pray for the people you need to confront and ask God to prepare their hearts. Ask Him to make them aware of their actions even before you speak to them.

Once you break free from control, you are well on your way to being free from approval addiction. As you continue to find freedom and strength, you can begin to help others who struggle with the same problems you have had.

PART 5

Moving into a Great Future

CHAPTER
20

Put Your Pain to Good Use

There is no way to get through life without experiencing pain. But it does not have to be wasted. No matter what happens in our lives, if we will keep praying and trusting God, keep loving Him and walking in His will to the best of our ability, He will cause everything to work out for good (see Romans 8:28). Whatever happened to us in the past may not have been good in and of itself, and it may have led to a struggle with acceptance and a desire for approval, but because God is good, He can take a difficult and painful situation and cause it to work out for our good and the good of others.

God's Purpose Is beyond Our Comprehension

The only monument in the world built in the shape of a bug—to honor a bug—is located in Enterprise, Alabama.

In 1915, the Mexican boll weevil invaded southeast Alabama and destroyed 60 percent of the cotton crop. In desperation, the farmers turned to planting peanuts. By 1917, the peanut industry had become so profitable that the county harvested more peanuts than any county in the nation. In gratitude, the people of the town erected a statue and inscribed these words: "In profound appreciation of the boll weevil, and what it has done to herald prosperity."

The instrument of their suffering had become the means of their blessing.

God is a God of purpose. We may not always understand His purpose, but we can be sure He definitely has one. Something may initially look terrible to us, and yet all the while God intends to show His glory by working something good from it.

We see an example of this truth in the biblical account of the death of Lazarus (see John 11:1–44). Lazarus was sick, so his sisters, Mary and Martha, sent a message to Jesus saying, "He whom You love [so well] is sick" (v. 3). When Jesus received the message, He said the sickness would not lead to death but had happened so God might be glorified. Instead of going to Lazarus while he was sick and healing him, Jesus waited until he died. By the time Jesus arrived, Lazarus had been in the grave for four days. Jesus raised Lazarus from the dead. He could have kept him from dying, but He let him die so people could see the miracle-working power of God and know that nothing is too hard for Him.

We wonder sometimes why God waits so long to come to our rescue or why He allows certain things to take place. We cannot always figure out what God is doing or why He is doing it, but if we trust Him, He will make something wonderful from it. God has a purpose for you, too. No matter what you have been through, He is healing you and making you ready to help others.

Hurt, Healed, and Ready to Help

Joseph's brothers hurt and rejected him, and we know from God's Word that the brothers were jealous of him because his father favored him. They sold him into slavery and told his father that wild animals had killed him. He was taken to Egypt, where he spent thirteen years in prison for a crime he did not commit (see Genesis 37–41).

But God was with Joseph, and he was able to interpret dreams. Egypt's ruler, Pharaoh, had a dream that Joseph interpreted, and he released him from prison. Joseph went to work for Pharaoh and was put in charge of everything; basically, he was the administrator of the whole country. During a great famine, Joseph was in a position to save multitudes of people, including his father and his brothers, who had treated him so cruelly.

This story is one of the most encouraging in the Bible. It teaches us the power of a good attitude during hard times. We see that no matter where we are, God can give us favor. We also see the power of forgiveness when

Joseph was willing to feed his brothers, who had hurt him so badly. The Bible says God's ways are past finding out (see Romans 11:33). We may not always understand, but we can trust.

Joseph had been hurt, but he was healed and stood ready to help. His struggles made him a better person, not a bitter person. Just think how different his life could have been had he refused to maintain a godly attitude all the way through his ordeal.

When we read about people in the Bible and the things they endured, we don't always think about the emotions they must have experienced. We read their stories almost as though the people are fictional characters—but they were real people just like you and me. They felt all the same emotions we would feel in their situations.

Ruth's husband died. I am sure that hurt her terribly. No doubt she was lonely, yet she chose to take care of her mother-in-law, an elderly woman named Naomi whom she accompanied to her homeland. Once there, they had very little provision, so Ruth had to glean in the wheat fields in order for them to eat. She ended up marrying a man named Boaz, who was extremely wealthy. As a result, Ruth and Naomi were provided with everything they needed. In addition, by bearing a son to Boaz, Ruth became part of the ancestral bloodline of Jesus (see Matthew 1:5).

My point in recounting these stories is that Joseph, Ruth, and many others suffered pain, received healing, and went on to help others.

Have you been hurt by someone or something? If so, you can make the same choice these people made. Don't spend your life angry and bitter; don't allow your emotional pain to imprison you in a lifelong struggle with approval. Receive healing and comfort from God, and then go on to help someone else. Don't waste your pain.

During World War II, Corrie ten Boom and her sister, Betsie, were held in a horrible concentration camp called Ravensbruck. They saw and suffered terrible torments, including starvation and nakedness in below-freezing temperatures. Betsie actually starved to death. During their time there, however, they continually encouraged other prisoners. They kept an attitude of praise, and eventually Corrie was released from the concentration camp through a clerical error.

After her release, she traveled the world telling of her experiences and the faithfulness of God. Her ministry surely became more powerful and effective than it would have been without her trials and suffering. Her life and ministry inspired and comforted millions. Although Corrie had been badly hurt, she allowed God to heal her, and she went on to help others.

As I have mentioned, I was abused and hurt very badly. When I was a young woman in my early twenties, I could never remember being happy or really feeling safe. I spent many years angry, bitter, and resentful. I am thankful that I learned to receive God's comfort and healing and that I am now able to help other people. I have experience with suffering, and I have had to learn many lessons, so I am able to help others through difficult situations and teach them what God has taught me.

Experienced Help Wanted

Have you ever needed a job, but every employment ad you read called for someone with experience? God also wants experienced help. When we go to work for God in His kingdom, He will use everything in our past, no matter how painful it was. He considers it experience. We have gone through some difficult things, and those things qualify us to help take someone else through them, too.

Take a look at how you can use your pain for someone else's gain. Can your mess become your ministry? Maybe you have gone through so much that you feel you have enough experience to be a specialist in some area. I am a specialist in overcoming shame, guilt, poor self-image, lack of confidence, fear, anger, bitterness, self-pity, and other negative situations. Press past your pain and get your "master's degree" so you can work in the kingdom for the One Who Is the Master of restoring hurting people, and be a blessing to others.

CHAPTER
21

Be a Blessing

Our daughter Sandra once dreaded seeing a certain person because that person had not been kind to her in the past. As she struggled with negative thoughts about the upcoming encounter, God spoke to her heart and said, "You don't need to be concerned about how others treat you; your concern should be how you treat them."

This message had a strong impact on Sandra and on me. How true it is. We are so concerned about how we are being treated that we have little or no concern for how we treat others. I agree that it is difficult not to be concerned that others who have treated us badly in the past will do so again. That is why it is so important not to think about it. We can deposit ourselves with God and trust Him to take care of us (see 1 Peter 4:19). He is our Vindicator (see Job 19:25), and as long as we behave properly toward others, including our enemies, God will bring a reward into our lives.

Because of what God had spoken to Sandra's heart, she

approached the meeting with a totally different attitude. She concentrated on being nice to the person who had not been nice to her previously. She made an effort to be encouraging and to show interest in the other person. She reported to me that the results were quite amazing. She spent several days with that person, and never once did she feel mistreated in any way.

The Bible says we are to "be mindful to be a blessing" (Galatians 6:10). That means we are to have our minds full of ways we can help others, as Sandra did. When our minds are filled with ways to be a blessing, we have no time to dwell on personal problems. It gives God an opportunity to work on them for us.

Healing First

You may be thinking, *I've been hurt and I want to help others, but I need healing first!* I often use the motto: "Hurt, healed, and ready to help!" Healing is vital. Many wounded people are in ministry today and they are trying to heal others, but ignoring their own pain. The blind cannot lead the blind; if they try to do so, they will both fall into a ditch (see Matthew 15:14). Trying to help others while ignoring our own problems never turns out well for anyone. This doesn't mean we can't be used at all to help people, because we definitely can, but we should not ignore our own need for healing. Part of our own healing can be reaching out to others, but we should not use "helping others" as an escape from our problems.

"How does our healing come?" We need the help of the Great Physician. We need His presence in our lives. Spending time with God is the most vital thing we can do, especially when we have been wounded.

We must spend time reading and studying God's Word, because it has the inherent power to heal. The Bible says we are to attend to God's Word, because it brings health and healing to all our flesh (see Proverbs 4:22). Our emotions and our minds are part of what the Bible calls "the flesh." According to Psalm 119:130, the entrance of God's Word brings light, which is something many of us are missing. We don't always see what we need to do. Often we don't even see our own problems. We think everyone else has a problem, and if they would all change, everything would be fine. We need light from God to understand ourselves, and light comes from His Word.

As I began my healing journey with God, His Holy Spirit started leading me into truth. Truth is another way to describe light. There were many things I did not understand. I didn't understand why I felt certain ways in certain situations or about certain types of people. My lack of light brought confusion into my life. It contributed to my negative feelings about myself. I didn't like many of my ways, but I could do nothing about them because I was in the dark. I was trapped! I didn't like the things I did; I didn't understand them, but I kept on doing them.

As truth and light came to me through God's Word, I realized that I sometimes interacted with others in certain ways not because I was a mean person, as the enemy had tried to make me believe; I was simply frightened. I had developed a complex system of ways to protect and take care of myself. I knew how to manipulate almost any situation to make sure no one took advantage of me. Yet I was tired of trying to protect and take care of myself all the time. I said I wanted someone to take care of me, but when anyone tried, I would not allow it. I wouldn't even let God take care of me. But His light set me free. Little by little He showed me things that opened my eyes and heart, and allowed change to come.

All healing is a process that takes time; this is especially true for emotional healing. It may not all be easy. Spending time with God in His Word and in His presence are the two main ingredients of being healed after being hurt.

Help Somebody on Purpose

While you are letting God work in your own life, use your pain. Be aggressive in helping others. Don't wait until you feel like doing so. Don't wait for some supernatural sign that God wants to use you. Just get started. God will use you in your world, with the people you are around in your daily life. What you make happen for someone else, God will make happen for you. Every seed you have sown into someone else's life represents a harvest you will reap in your own life—especially in your pursuit to overcome approval addiction.

Don't waste your pain. Let it be someone else's gain!

Conclusion

We all want to feel satisfied. We all want contentment. We all want to know we are loved and accepted for who we are. We may think acceptance and approval from people will make us feel complete. However, the Bible teaches us that when we trust in people to give us what only God can give, we live under a curse; but when we believe, trust in, and rely on the Lord, we are blessed (see Jeremiah 17:5–8). The joy, peace, and fulfillment we seek come from being filled with God, and nothing else.

I encourage you to read the Book of Ecclesiastes, written by a man named Solomon, who tried literally everything to find this kind of deep inner completeness and satisfaction. Nothing he tried worked until he came full circle and realized what he truly wanted had been available to him all the time. He wanted God!

If you have never accepted Jesus as your Savior, that is a good starting point. But even that won't fix everything in you and in your life unless you also accept Him as your Lord. Jesus intends to be everything to us. He does nothing halfway. He will never be satisfied to have one little corner of our lives. He wants the run of the entire house. As believers in Jesus, we are His home, and nothing should be off-limits to Him.

It took me years of chasing after things to discover that I had what I needed all along. I was complete in Jesus Christ (see Colossians 2:10). All I needed to do was believe it!

As I bring this book to a close, my desire is to leave you feeling complete, satisfied, and fulfilled. I don't want you to feel empty or frustrated and to continue looking for something to fill that emptiness, something that will only add to the pain you may already be experiencing.

Receive What You've Been Given

Know who you are in Jesus, and understand your righteousness (your right standing with God), which is found only in Christ. Everything you need is available for the taking. All you have to do is receive by faith what Jesus has already provided.

Let faith take the lead, and feelings will follow. First, you must believe that God loves you; affirm it to yourself daily through meditating on it and speaking it. Your feelings will come later. Start believing you have been made acceptable in Jesus. Ask Him for favor with the right people, and don't worry about the ones who do not seem to value you. They are missing out, because actually you are a great person, and a relationship with you is something to be greatly desired!

God does not want you to be tormented by the disapproval of other people; rather, He wants you to rejoice in His approval. He loves you! You are a special and unique individual, and He has a wonderful plan for your life. Don't let people or the enemy steal it from you.

Meditate on your position in Christ according to God's Word, not according to what people think and say about you. Remember that people had terrible things to say about Jesus, and they rejected Him, yet the Bible says, "The stone which the builders rejected has become the chief cornerstone" (Psalm 118:22).

I believe God is doing something wonderful in you and will continue to do something wonderful through you. Live to please God, not people. You have His approval, and that is all you really need!

ABOUT THE AUTHOR

JOYCE MEYER is one of the world's leading practical Bible teachers. Her TV and radio broadcast, *Enjoying Everyday Life,* airs on hundreds of television networks and radio stations worldwide.

Joyce has written more than 100 inspirational books. Her bestsellers include *God Is Not Mad at You*; *Making Good Habits, Breaking Bad Habits*; *Do Yourself a Favor...Forgive*; *Living Beyond Your Feelings*; *Power Thoughts*; *Battlefield of the Mind*; *Look Great, Feel Great*; *The Confident Woman*; *I Dare You*; and *Never Give Up!*

Joyce travels extensively, holding conferences throughout the year, speaking to thousands around the world.

JOYCE MEYER MINISTRIES
U.S. & FOREIGN OFFICE ADDRESSES

Joyce Meyer Ministries
P.O. Box 655
Fenton, MO 63026
USA
(636) 349-0303

Joyce Meyer Ministries—Canada
P.O. Box 7700
Vancouver, BC V6B 4E2
Canada
(800) 868-1002

Joyce Meyer Ministries—Australia
Locked Bag 77
Mansfield Delivery Centre
Queensland 4122
Australia
(07) 3349 1200

Joyce Meyer Ministries—England
P.O. Box 1549
Windsor SL4 1GT
United Kingdom
(0) 1753 831102

Joyce Meyer Ministries—South Africa
P.O. Box 5
Cape Town 8000
South Africa
(27) 21-701-1056

OTHER BOOKS BY JOYCE MEYER

DEVOTIONALS

Battlefield of the Mind Devotional
The Confident Woman Devotional
*Ending Your Day Right**
Hearing from God Each Morning
Love Out Loud
New Day, New You
Power Thoughts Devotional
*Starting Your Day Right**
Trusting God Day By Day

* Also available in Spanish